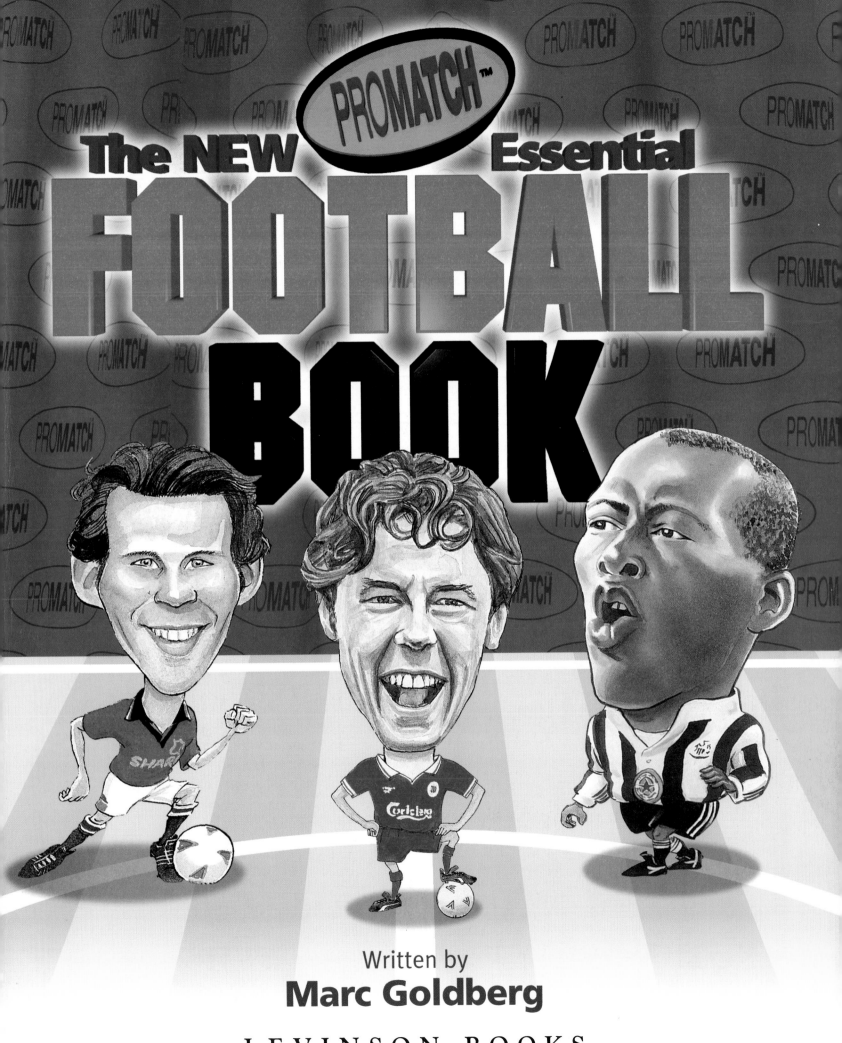

The NEW PROMATCH™ Essential FOOTBALL BOOK

Written by

Marc Goldberg

LEVINSON BOOKS

First Published in Great Britain by Levinson Books Ltd in 1997

10 9 8 7 6 5 4 3 2 1

A CIP record for this title is available from the British Library.

ISBN 1-86233-087-5

Printed and bound in Italy

Contents

PREMIERSHIP REVIEW 1997/98

Half a decade of the Premiership has brought so many thrills and plenty of excitement; justifying the boast that the Premiership is the most exciting in the world.

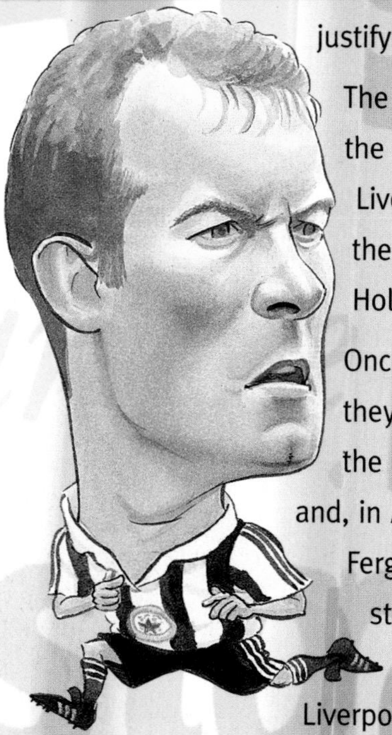

The 1996/97 title race didn't quite go down to the wire but going into the final week there were still three teams - Manchester United, Liverpool and Newcastle - who still had a chance of glory. But at the bottom of the table there was a dramatic climax that even a Hollywood scriptwriter would have struggled to make credible!

Once again Manchester United won the Premiership although they were closely pursued by Liverpool and Arsenal. But it was the Old Trafford Reds who crucially had the strongest squad and, in Alex Ferguson, the most battle hardened manager. Alex Ferguson and his team always looked as though they could step up a gear if they had to and, when the time came, they did. On Merseyside they won 3-1 against Liverpool near the end of the season, proving their capability to give the right performance on the big occasion. This victory virtually ensured their fourth Premiership title in five years. Schmeichel, Beckham and Solskjaer were outstanding though Old Trafford god, Eric Cantona rarely hit the heights. He left at the end of the season.

Although they were pipped by Newcastle, Liverpool and Arsenal spent the latter half of the season scrapping for second place and both showed improvements on past seasons. The influence of Arsene Wenger at Highbury proved highly productive with signs of a more continental style of football being played by a side not known for its finesse. Roy Evans persisted with the orthodox Liverpool style, that of patient, precision passing, but there were signs, particularly away from home, of more grit and determination.

There were plenty of other things that made the headlines at the right end of the table. Second-placed Newcastle started the campaign well, with Shearer effortlessly hitting the form that has made him one of the best in the world, but their season was turned upside down by the January

Premiership Review

resignation of Kevin Keegan. Kenny Dalglish was thought of as the perfect replacement and, despite qualifying for the Champions League, his plans won't really come to fruition until next season.

Aston Villa ground out enough results for fifth place and a UEFA Cup berth as they slowly climbed the table. David Pleat shrewdly marshalled Sheffield Wednesday to seventh, narrowly missing a European place.

Perhaps the highest profile team of the season was Chelsea, with their foreign stars, including the unbelievable talents of Gianfranco Zola. Ruud Gullit looks as though he's building a team that'll add consistency to the outstanding ability of Zola, Hughes and Di Matteo. They'll be looking to improve on their final position of sixth.

At the bottom it was the closest season for years. Nottingham Forest finished last and although they were surprise victims, they struggled to score goals all season leaving Stuart Pearce with a difficult job in his debut management season.

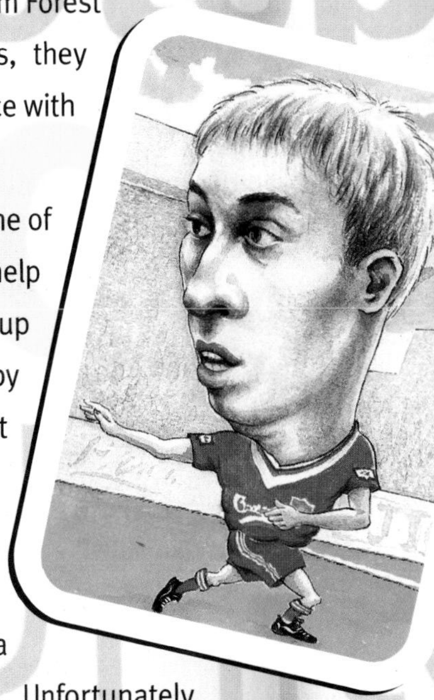

Ravanelli, Emerson and the magnificent Juninho - some of the world's most exciting players were unable to help Middlesbrough avoid the drop. Their pile up of cup games meant that their players became too weary by the end of the season. Ultimately they could just not take the pace.

Sunderland filled the third relegation spot, proving that a team can have all the fighting spirit and determination but they still need a certain amount of quality to stay in the Premiership. Unfortunately Sunderland just did not have enough players of Premiership standard.

During the new season there are going to be many changes, with new players coming from abroad and the likes of Bolton and Barnsley battling against the odds to stay in the Premiership. Yet it is the top of the league which will dominate the nation's attention. It is difficult to see beyond last season's top four - Manchester United, Newcastle, Arsenal and Liverpool - battling it out again in what should be the most keenly contested title race in years.

Paul Merson

Striker

Place of Birth London, England
Height 1.83m
Date of Birth 20/03/68
Weight 78kg

After his well documented troubles outside football he got down to hard work and has found himself playing some of the best football of his life. While Paul had a lay off from the game many expected it would take a long time for him to get back into the swing of things; instead he played over 50 games in a row and it was finally an injury that forced him to rest!

His sparkling performances have lifted the Gunners on many an occasion and his positive attacking play has helped Arsenal lose some of their 'Boring Arsenal' tag.

Glenn Hoddle has been just as impressed with 'The Merse' as have many other football fans. Indeed Hoddle gave Paul another chance on the international scene where it seems that he will compete with Steve McManaman for a place in the England side.

Player to Watch

Patrick Vieira

Midfielder

Place of Birth Dakar, Senegal
Height 1.91m
Date of Birth 02/06/76
Weight 76kg

After only 22 minutes of his debut the Highbury crowd were chanting Patrick's name. Not surprising really. He's a typical fan's favourite; young, hard working, he demonstrates plenty of effort and most of all a clear love for his new club.

Costing £3.5 million he was a player that few in England had heard of when he arrived from the giants of Milan, but much was expected from the surprise package.

He is a player Arsenal have longed for. With his all round football ability and an unbelievably classy touch for someone over six feet tall, he is a great prospect for the future, not only for his club but also for the French national team.

Dennis Bergkamp

Striker

Place of Birth Amsterdam, The Netherlands
Height 1.83m
Date of Birth 18/05/69
Weight 78kg

The former Ajax and Inter Milan forward seems to have settled in now and has become a firm favourite with the Highbury crowd. Even though his goalscoring has hardly been prolific since his arrival, his countless assists and deft touches of skill make the £7.5 million paid for him worth every penny.

His partnership with Ian Wright has resulted in a combination of fine skill and deadly finishing. Arsenal's all round build-up play is now so much more entertaining.

Now a regular on the Dutch side, he will be looking to put one over his French club manager when the 98 World Cup comes around in France. He'll be hoping to help The Netherlands shake their 'non-achievers' tag.

Arsenal

Tony Adams

Defender

Place of Birth	London, England
Height	1.86m
Date of Birth	10/10/66
Weight	87kg

Even though injury problems have prevented Tony from having his usual outstanding season, when he was available he again showed why he is so highly rated and is still England's first choice centre back.

His partnership with fellow defenders Bould, Dixon, Keown and Winterburn stretches back over seven years and even though there has been talk that new blood will be brought in to bolster an old yet capable defence, there has never been any question over Tony's place in the team.

Now over 30 years old he gets the usual newspaper criticism that he is past his best but he is a player who's been mentioned alongside Moore and Beckenbauer and other greats. Players like that do not fade away with age.

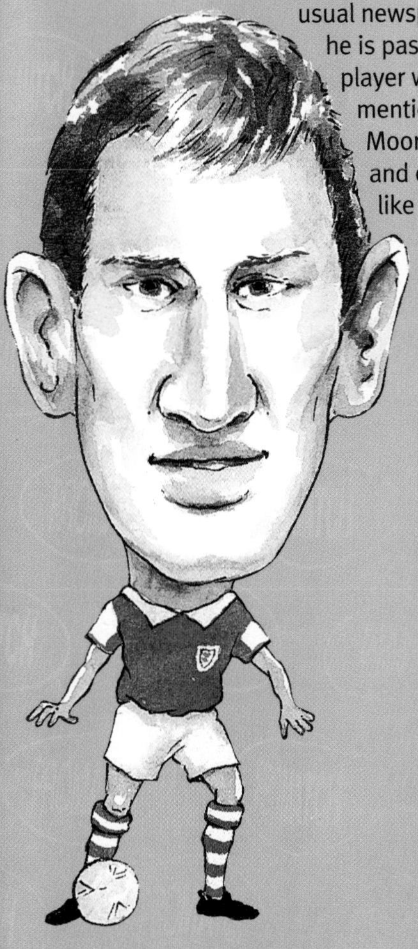

Player of the Season

Ian Wright

Striker

Place of Birth	Woolwich, England
Height	1.75m
Date of Birth	03/11/63
Weight	73kg

Nearing the age of 33 critics and pundits everywhere had the gall to write off Ian Wright at the start of the 96/97 Premiership season - despite his near century of League goals for the club. How he made those critics eat their words.

Finishing in the scoring charts alongside the likes of Shearer, Ferdinand and Fowler is nothing new for the former Palace marksman. But his partnership with Deadly Dennis Bergkamp has given Ian a different role. He said: 'Dennis is great to play with, he is one of these strikers who gives me the responsibility over scoring the goals while he makes the running off the ball and sets up the chances. It is great!'

Many still feel that a replacement should be found for Ian, but I think he has proved to his manager Arsene Wenger that he is well worth his place and will be a threat for at least another season.

David Seaman

Goalkeeper

Place of Birth	Rotherham, England
Height	1.93m
Date of Birth	19/09/63
Weight	93kg

After suffering an injury at Old Trafford last season – a game which also saw Arsenal lose their grip on the championship race – David suffered an erratic season for first team appearances. Yet he still remains England's number one and possibly Arsenal's most prized asset.

After Euro 96 he had established himself as the best goalkeeper in the country and probably Europe. His reflexes, judgement, and inspiration make him a player who sets a great example for those learning the game.

With a continental manager and changes at Highbury unforeseeable, David's place is one position that's not under threat. He is a player that many managers around the world would like in their side, and the Gunners are extremely unlikely to let him go.

Arsenal

STATS & FACTS

Club Details

Manager: Arsene Wenger

Assistant Manager: Pat Rice

Captain: Tony Adams

Colours: Home - Red and White

Away - Navy and Teal

Ground: Highbury

Capacity: 38,500

CLUB HONOURS

League
Champions - 1930-31, 1932-33, 1933-34, 1934-35, 1937-38, 1947-48, 1952-53, 1970-71, 1988-89, 1990-91

FA Cup
Winners - 1930, 1936, 1950, 1971, 1979, 1993

League Cup
Winners - 1987, 1993

European Cup Winners Cup
Winners - 1994

UEFA Cup Winners - 1970

What are their chances?

With a solid foundation and the likes of Vieira, Hughes and Anelka coming through there is a great blend of youth and experience. Now with a manager who's shown other Premiership managers that travelling the world for new talent can work, Arsenal are being regarded as one of the major contenders for the 97/98 season.

With the challenge of another European campaign there is plenty to look forward to, and it is certainly within their capabilities to make a name for themselves in Europe and again challenge Manchester United and Liverpool for the title.

PAST RECORD

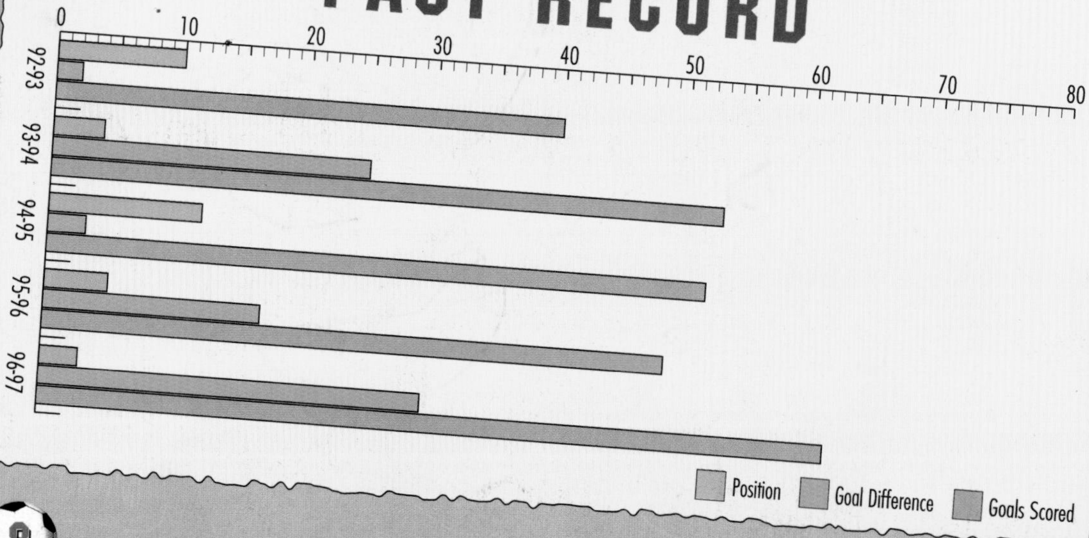

TITLE ODDS

5/1

ON AUGUST 9TH START OF SEASON

Arsenal

TEAM POSITIONS AND LINE-UP

1	DAVID SEAMAN
2	LEE DIXON
3	NIGEL WINTERBURN
4	PATRICK VIEIRA
5	STEVE BOULD
6	TONY ADAMS
7	DAVID PLATT
8	IAN WRIGHT
9	PAUL MERSON
10	DENNIS BERGKAMP
11	NICHOLAS ANELKA
12	
13	
14	MARTIN KEOWN
15	RAY PARLOUR
16	
17	
18	
19	REMI GARDE
20	CHRIS KIWOMYA
21	
22	IAN SELLY
23	
24	JOHN LUKIC
25	SCOTT MARSHALL
26	LEE HARPER
27	PAUL SHAW
28	STEPHEN HUGHES
29	ADRIAN CLARKE
30	
31	MATTHEW ROSE
32	
33	
34	
35	
36	

Dwight Yorke

Striker

Place of Birth Tobago
Height 1.80m
Date of Birth 03/11/71
Weight 76kg

When visiting Villa Park one thing that's immediately obvious is the fans' absolute devotion to their hero, Dwight Yorke. This is highlighted by the fact that he has his own song, sung to the tune of Frank Sinatra's 'New York, New York', changing the words to 'Dwight Yorke, Dwight Yorke'!

He has earned the right to be adored by the Villa faithful, with his electrifying forward play and an abundance of goals that have helped Villa to be looked upon once again as one of the Premiership's top sides.

At 25 it seems as though he has been on the scene for a while but after signing a new long term contract he obviously believes his club will push for another crack at the title.

Steve Staunton

Defender

Place of Birth Drogheda, Eire
Height 1.83m
Date of Birth 19/01/69
Weight 78kg

Having suffered several injuries over the past few seasons he has once again found the form that saw him being talked about as one of the best full-backs in the country.

Yet this season he has been chosen to play in a three-man central defensive system. Alongside Ehiogu and Southgate, Steve adds a bit of flair and skill to the other's strength.

Still one of the first choice players in the Eire side, he has become one of Mick McCarthy's most reliable players in a national side which has recently failed to live up to its potential.

Player to Watch

Julian Joachim

Striker

Place of Birth Peterborough, England
Height 1.68m
Date of Birth 20/09/74
Weight 74kg

After a full season at Aston Villa first team opportunities have been limited for Julian, yet he has shown on many an occasion that he certainly has the ability to match his manager's faith in him.

His speed and turn of pace along with tricky feet have tormented defences and have given many defenders torrid Saturday afternoons.

At only 23 he is still to make his mark in the Premiership but many believe that the 97/98 season will be his year, and it looks as though he may be played in his preferred winger's role rather than as a striker.

Aston Villa

Stan Collymore

Striker

Place of Birth	Stone, England
Height	1.83m
Date of Birth	22/01/71
Weight	82kg

After an indifferent and often controversial spell at Liverpool, Stan will welcome the chance to play for the club he supported as a boy. He will hope to delight the Villa faithful.

His £7 million move brought his transfer fee tally to £18 million, making him one of the most valuable players in the Premiership.

Brian Little is a manager who takes no nonsense and that may well be a good thing for Stan who has been able to get away with things in the past – being late for training, refusing to play for the reserves – that he should never have got away with.

Player of the Season

Ugo Ehiogu

Defender

Place of Birth	London, England
Height	1.88m
Date of Birth	03/11/72
Weight	84kg

A towering influence at the centre of the defence, his menacing runs forward and determined tackling have made him one of the most highly rated defenders in the country.

Already noticed at international level, he has even been mentioned in the same category as players like Terry Butcher and Alan Hansen.

Very noticeable on the pitch, with his bright yellow hair, he tends to be one of the unsung heroes but with time definitely on his side he could become one of the all time great centre backs at Villa Park.

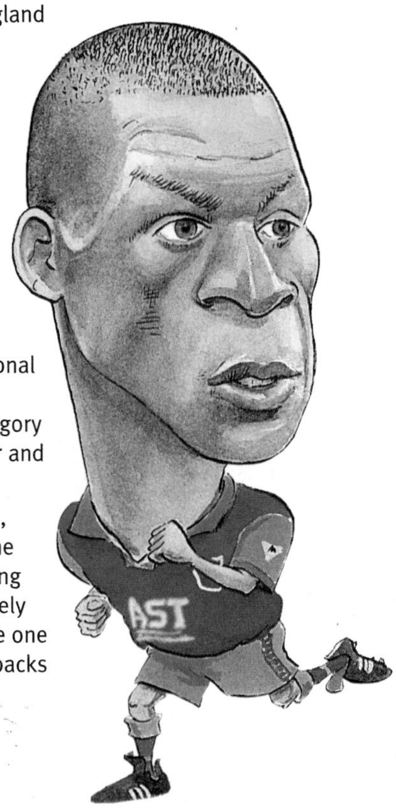

Gareth Southgate

Defender

Place of Birth	Watford, England
Height	1.78m
Date of Birth	03/09/70
Weight	75kg

Many thought that Gareth would take quite a while to deal with the penalty miss disappointment of Euro 96 yet he showed those that doubted him that he had the character to play just as well, maybe even better, in the season following the European Championships.

For a midfielder turned centre back his composure on the ball is to be admired. He also shows great professionalism on and off the pitch, gaining enormous amounts of respect and admiration from girls and boys who are learning the game.

His sense of humour is also apparent with his appearances on television and, along with some sturdy performances for club and country, he looks an absolute bargain for the £2 million Brian Little paid for him.

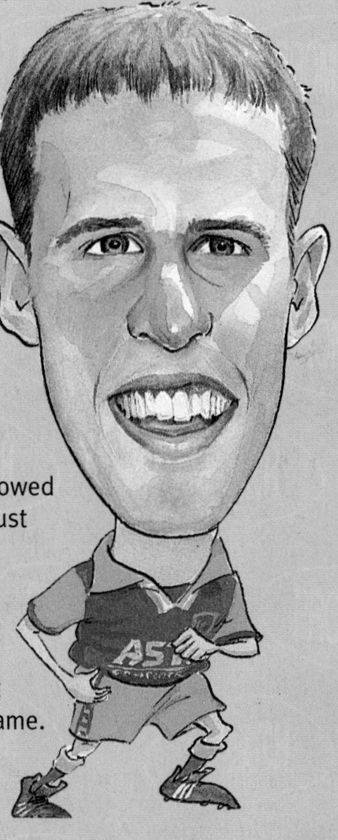

Aston Villa

STATS & FACTS

Club Details

Manager: Brian Little

Assistant Manager: Allan Evans

Captain: Andy Townsend

Colours: Home - Claret and Blue

Away - White and Claret

Ground: Villa Park

Capacity: 39,339

CLUB HONOURS

League
Champions - 1893-94, 1895-96, 1896-97, 1898-99, 1899-1900, 1909-10, 1980-81

FA Cup
Winners - 1887, 1895, 1897, 1905, 1913, 1920, 1957

League Cup
Winners - 1961, 1975, 1977, 1994, 1996

European Cup
Winners - 1982

European Super Cup
Winners - 1983

What are their chances?

Brian Little has built a team that has plenty of strength and determination yet lacks that cutting edge to sustain a push for the championship.

Despite fresh faces coming into the club, I believe that Villa are still only good enough for the European place which they now take for granted.

Now Brian Little has learned about European football he may well progress far in the UEFA Cup - Villa's best bet for success.

PAST RECORD

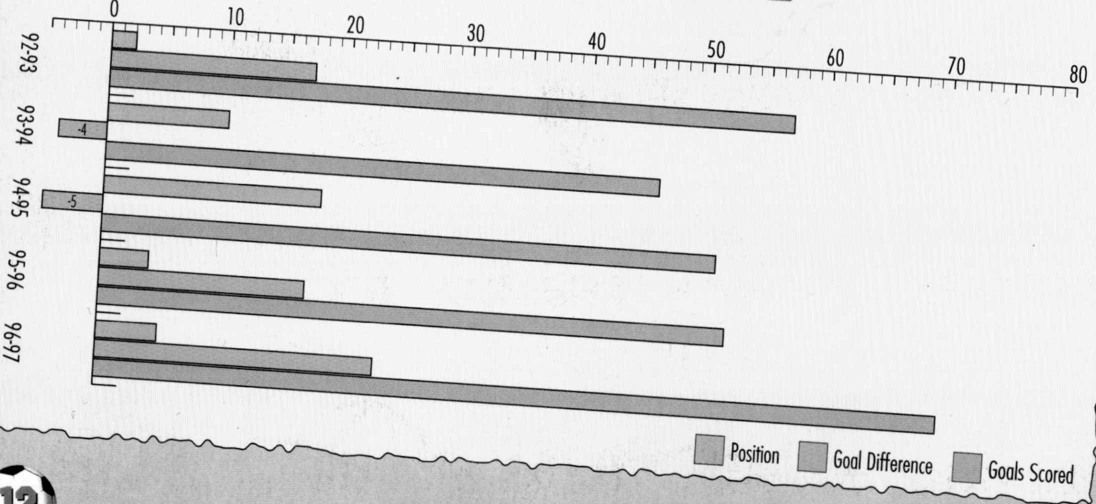

TITLE ODDS
20/1
ON AUGUST 9TH START OF SEASON

Aston Villa

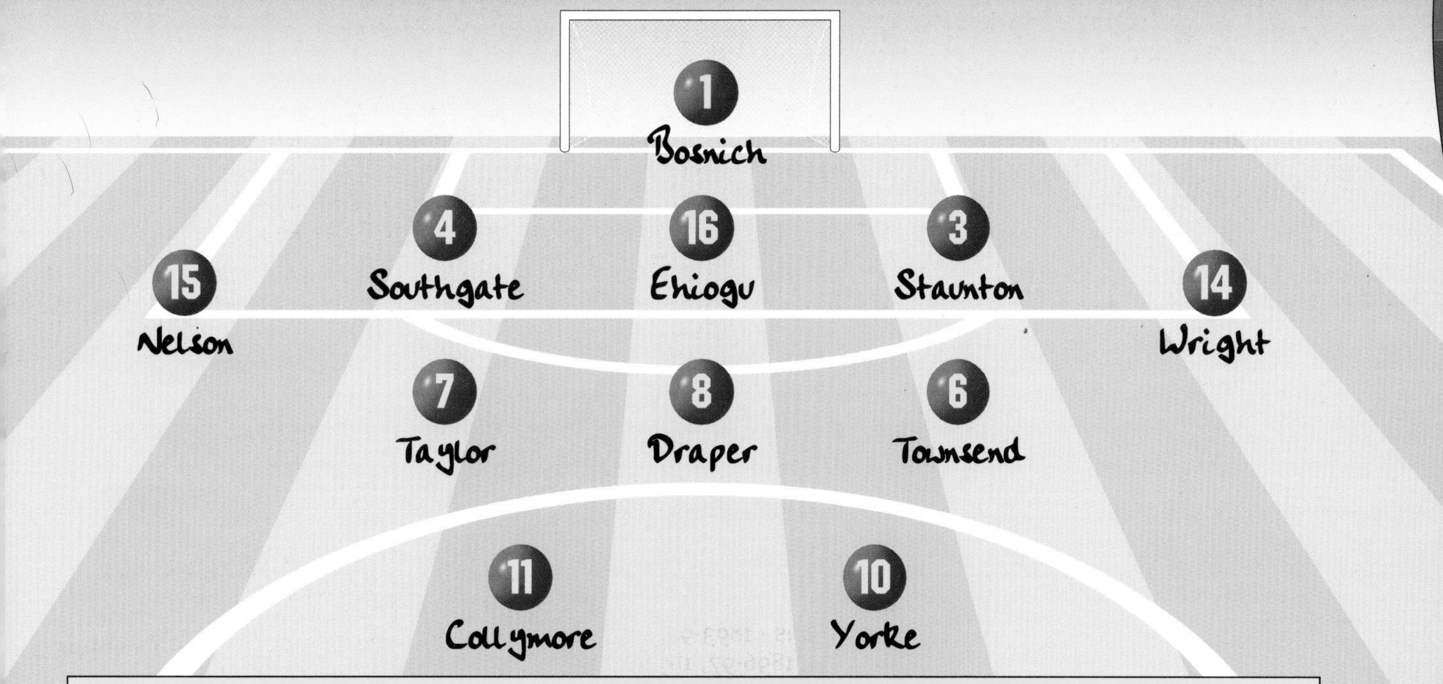

TEAM POSITIONS AND LINE-UP

1	MARK BOSNICH
2	GARY CHARLES
3	STEVE STAUNTON
4	GARETH SOUTHGATE
5	
6	ANDY TOWNSEND
7	IAN TAYLOR
8	MARK DRAPER
9	SAVO MILOSEVIC
10	DWIGHT YORKE
11	STAN COLLYMORE
12	JULIAN JOACHIM
13	MICHAEL OAKES
14	ALAN WRIGHT
15	FERNANDO NELSON
16	UGO EHIOGU
17	LEE HENDRIE
18	
19	GARETH FARRELLY
20	RICCARDO SCIMECA
21	
22	
23	NEIL DAVIS
24	SCOTT MURRAY
25	
26	SASA CURCIC
27	
28	
29	
30	ADAM RACHEL
31	
32	
33	
34	
35	
36	

Matty Appleby

Defender

Place of Birth	Middlesbrough, England
Height	1.80m
Date of Birth	16/04/72
Weight	75kg

Having made 20 appearances for Newcastle before the Magpies were the star-studded team they are now, Matty hopes that he can return to St. James Park and show those who remember him that he is well worth his place in the Premiership.

After missing out in the playoffs in 96 with Darlington, he was quickly snapped up by Danny Wilson who gave Matty his chance in the First Division where he has been one of the most consistent defenders in the league.

He has speed, tenacity and a lot of class about his game and, having played in the lower leagues, he has a wealth of experience and is now at the point where he feels the challenge of Premiership football has come just at the right time in his career.

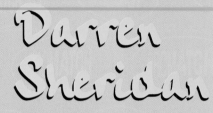

Darren Sheridan

Midfielder

Place of Birth	Manchester, England
Height	1.72m
Date of Birth	08/12/67
Weight	61kg

Having joined from non-league Winsford four seasons ago, Darren has come on in leaps and bounds and was one of the most tricky wingers in the First Division.

A player with plenty of talent and great pace though he can sometimes drift in and out of games which can lead to him occasionally being dropped by his workmanlike manager, Danny Wilson.

A player who, on last season's form, should find it comparatively easy to bridge the gap between First Division and Premiership football.

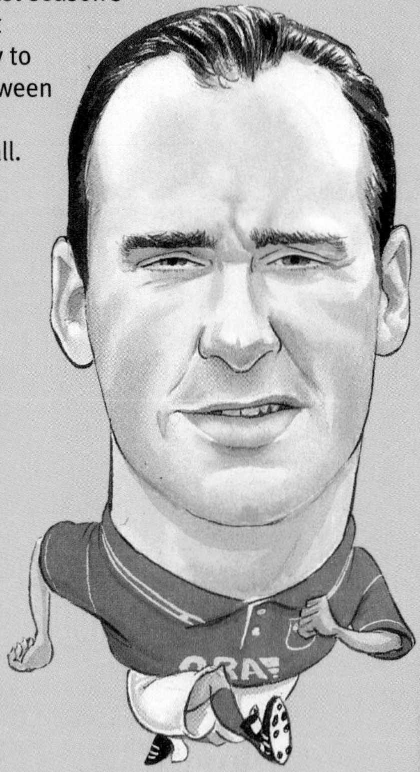

Player to Watch

Andy Liddell

Striker

Place of Birth	Leeds, England
Height	1.74m
Date of Birth	28/06/73
Weight	64kg

Much has been said about this young Scot who has been likened to his idol Kenny Dalglish. He has a lot of the same qualities as the Newcastle manager and hopes that he can have some of the success that Kenny had as a player. Although short of stature and a bit lightweight, he has tremendous pace and a real eye for goal. Having been capped at Under-21 level for Scotland he is hoping that in his first full season in the Premiership he will be able to impress not only Premiership fans but also Scotland manager Craig Brown. His manager Danny Wilson is very hopeful that Andy will score the goals that can help Barnsley defy all the pundits and survive their first season in the top flight.

David Watson

Goalkeeper

Place of Birth	Barnsley, England
Height	1.79m
Date of Birth	10/11/73
Weight	73kg

Being regarded as one of the best young goalkeepers in the country over the last few years has been an accolade that David must have loved, yet he now has the chance to justify all this lavish praise when he plays against top teams week in, week out.

At the prime age of 24 he has been a regular in the Barnsley goal for the past four years and he feels confident that he has the ability to attract the attention of Glenn Hoddle.

Although under six feet, he compensates for his lack of inches with tremendous reflexes and has been known to pull off breathtaking saves.

Player of the Season

Neil Redfearn

Midfielder

Place of Birth	Dewsbury, England
Height	1.75m
Date of Birth	20/06/65
Weight	76kg

True determination and enthusiasm are two adjectives which truly express Neil Redfearn's play. Neil uses such industrial attributes to make up for his lack of flair.

At the age of 32 he's captained his side to promotion, and though many may say that an unfashionable side like Barnsley do not belong in the top flight, few would argue with Neil's right to be there after the commitment he has shown his club in his 250-plus appearances.

Having played in the top division before with Oldham, albeit in a relegated side, he will undoubtedly do his best and give 110% to make sure that Barnsley stay afloat in the Premiership.

Barnsley

Martin Bullock

Midfielder

Place of Birth	Derby, England
Height	1.72m
Date of Birth	05/03/75
Weight	64kg

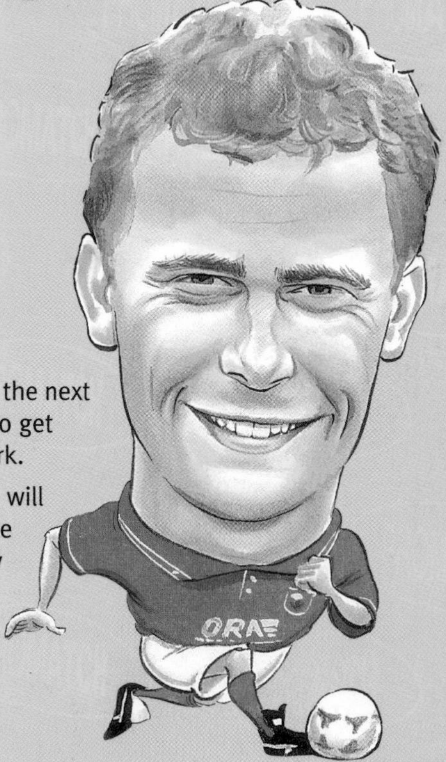

Martin is Barnsley through and through and has worked his way through the ranks to get to where he is today.

A workmanlike player who's being talked about as the next Paul Ince, due to his battling qualities and ability to get forward and score goals from the middle of the park.

There are many players in the Barnsley squad who will find themselves trying to keep their first team place in the Premiership yet Martin has youth and ability on his side and the only way he will be lost to Barnsley is if a big club comes in and takes him from the Tykes.

Barnsley

STATS & FACTS

Club Details

Manager: Danny Wilson

Assistant Manager: Eric Winstanley

Captain: Neil Redfearn

Colours: Home - Red and White

Away - Blue and Black

Ground: Oakwell

Capacity: 19,101

CLUB HONOURS

FA Cup
Winners - 1912

What are their chances?

There are many who feel that a club like Barnsley do not belong in the Premiership and that they will just become the whipping boys who every team will expect to beat. But Danny Wilson and his team fought their way into the division and will fight to stay in it.

There is a good blend of youth and experience and there will surely be additions to the squad. Yet at the end of the day Barnsley will struggle simply because they do not have enough players with Premiership experience.

TITLE ODDS
500/1
ON AUGUST 9TH
START OF SEASON

Barnsley

TEAM POSITIONS AND LINE-UP

1	2	3	4	5	6
DAVID WATSON	NICKY EADEN	DARREN SHERIDAN	MATTY APPLEBY	STEVE DAVIS	ARJAN DE ZEEUW
7	8	9	10	11	12
NEIL REDFEARN	ANDY LIDDELL	JOHN HENDRIE	PAUL WILKINSON	CLINT MARCELLE	MARTIN BULLOCK
13	14	15	16	17	18
ADAM SOLLITT	GOVAN BOSONCIC	CAREL VAN DER VELDAN	NEIL THOMPSON	SCOTT JONES	ADRIAN MOSES
19	20	21	22	23	24
GARY FLEMING	DAVE REGIS				
25	26	27	28	29	30
31	32	33	34	35	36

Tim Flowers

Goalkeeper

Place of Birth	Kenilworth, England
Height	1.88m
Date of Birth	03/02/67
Weight	89kg

After a nervous start to the new season, when Tim received as much criticism as the rest of the players, his confidence steadily increased and he is firmly back as a key member of Glenn Hoddle's World Cup preparations. Many fans from other clubs admire the former Southampton keeper because of the way he conducts himself on and off the pitch; it is very rare that you see him without a smile on his face.

Early season rumours that he was set to move from Blackburn have proved to be untrue, and, thanks to his presence, the Rovers defence became more solid in the last months of the season, especially at Ewood Park.

Graeme Le Saux

Defender

Place of Birth	Jersey, Channel Islands
Height	1.75m
Date of Birth	17/10/68
Weight	76kg

What began as a traumatic season for the former Chelsea man has ended on a much higher note, as he firmly re-established himself as one of the best left-backs in the country.

After a double leg break in 1995, few thought Graeme could regain his old form, however, the same critics are now suggesting that he has returned a better player and his price value has soared since his return.

He has always had a special place in the crowd's affections and even more fans are learning to respect Graeme, not only for his timing and tackling but for his obvious love of the game.

Player to Watch

Graham Fenton

Striker

Place of Birth	Wallsend, England
Height	1.78m
Date of Birth	22/5/74
Weight	74kg

Despite finishing the 95/96 season as the potential replacement to Shearer, and scoring a number of goals in the process, Fenton's rise to the top has been cut short by niggling injuries that kept him out for the first half of the 96/97 season.

After his performances for Blackburn and Aston Villa, few would argue that there are many youngsters with as much potential.

Fenton played for the same boys' club as Shearer in Newcastle and the similarities don't end there. Graham has pace, and, despite being short, he makes up for that with tenacity and dazzling skills.

Chris Sutton

Striker

Place of Birth	Nottingham, England
Height	1.91m
Date of Birth	10/03/73
Weight	77kg

Despite the departure of close friend and strike-partner, Alan Shearer, Chris has been one of the few bright spots in what has been quite a disappointing season for Blackburn Rovers.

He started the season still struggling to get over the injury which hampered his progress in the last two years but since his return, in October 96, the £5 million man has not looked back.

Not only was he one of the top marksmen for his club in the 96/97 season, he has shown that his all-round play has improved greatly, making him one of the most skilful 'big-men' in the Premiership.

Player of the Season

Colin Hendry

Defender

Place of Birth	Keith, Scotland
Height	1.86m
Date of Birth	07/12/65
Weight	76kg

Despite many saying that the 96/97 season was a very disappointing one for Blackburn Rovers there can be little doubt that Colin Hendry has continued in his role as the rock of the defence. Undoubtedly he was the player of the year again, rediscovering the form he showed when the Ewood Park side won the Premiership title.

His performances during the season motivated the entire team to succeed and guaranteed their Premiership survival, and his passion was witnessed by Craig Brown, who sees the blond star as an integral part of the World Cup squad looking to France in 1998. He looks set to lead his country across the Channel as the captain.

Kevin Gallacher

Striker

Place of Birth	Clydebank, Scotland
Height	1.70m
Date of Birth	23/11/66
Weight	71kg

The tiny Scot has discovered a new lease of life since the departure of Alan Shearer. Tony Parkes obviously knew that he had true class waiting in the wings to replace the £15 million man.

Deployed as a striker, or slightly behind the front two, it has been his partnership with Chris Sutton over the last half of the season that has won Kevin most praise.

Gallacher has also impressed Craig Brown, having managed to recapture his club form for his country. His goals will aid the Scottish cause as they strive to reach France in 1998.

Blackburn Rovers

STATS & FACTS

Club Details

Manager: Roy Hodgson

Assistant Manager: Tony Parkes

Captain: Colin Hendry

Colours: Home - Blue and White

Away - Yellow and Navy

Ground: Ewood Park

Capacity: 31,367

CLUB HONOURS

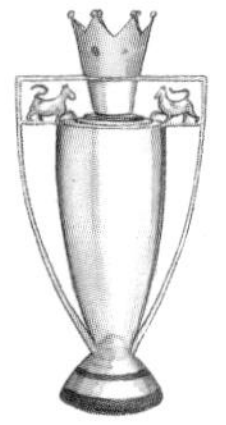

League
Champions - 1911-12, 1913-14, 1994-95

FA Cup
Winners - 1884, 1885, 1886, 1890, 1891, 1928

What are their chances?

With Alan Shearer leaving before the beginning of the 96/97 campaign, it left the club shell-shocked and really set the foundations for Rovers' most disappointing season in the Premiership.

Yet with a new cultured, knowledgable manager in Roy Hodgson there is now the know-how to bring in the right players. Hodgson will add something fresh to Blackburn's approach.

It is almost certain they will have a more successful season this year, but don't expect anything spectacular.

PAST RECORD

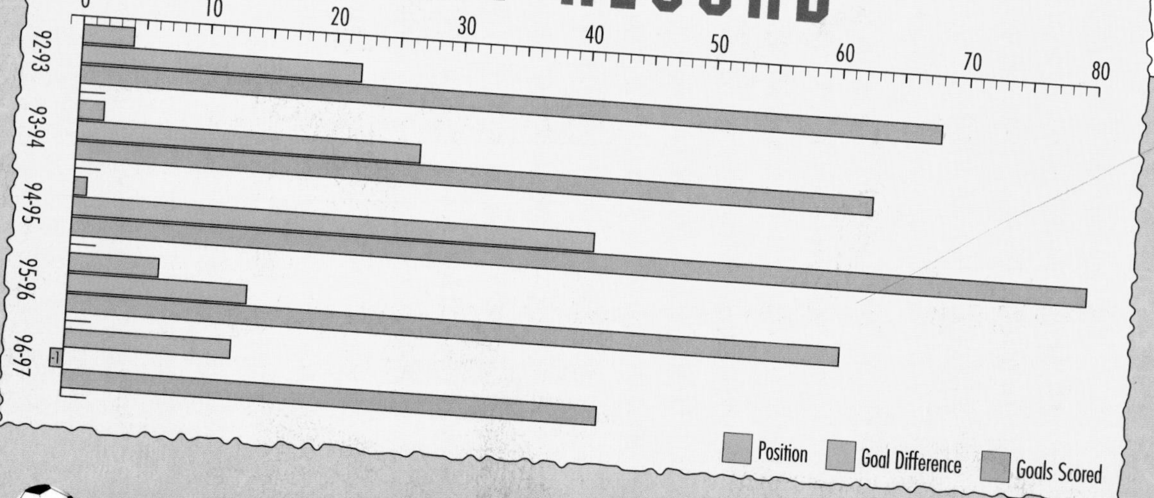

TITLE ODDS

50/1

ON AUGUST 9TH START OF SEASON

Blackburn Rovers

TEAM POSITIONS AND LINE-UP

1 TIM FLOWERS	2 CHRIS COLEMAN	3 JEFF KENNA	4 TIM SHERWOOD	5 COLIN HENDRY	6 GRAEME LE SAUX
7 STUART RIPLEY	8 KEVIN GALLACHER	9 CHRIS SUTTON	10 LARS BOHINEN	11 JASON WILCOX	12 NICKY MARKER
13 SHAY GIVEN	14 GRAHAM FENTON	15 MATT HOLMES	16 PER PEDERSON	17 BILLY MCKINLAY	18 NIKLAS GUDMUNDSSON
19 ADAM REED	20 HENNING BERG	21 GEOGIOUS DONIS	22 LARS BOHINEN	23 GARRY FLITCROFT	24 PAUL WARHURST
25 IAN PEARCE	26 MARLON BROOMES	27	28	29	30
31	32	33	34 GARY CROFT	35	36

Gudni Bergsson

Defender

Place of Birth	Reykjavik, Iceland
Height	1.85m
Date of Birth	21/07/65
Weight	84kg

Having had spells at Tottenham and then in his native Iceland, it seems that he has found his niche at Bolton where he captained the team to promotion as they stormed the First Division in 96/97.

A commanding figure in the box; his partnerships with Gerry Taggart and Chris Fairclough brushed aside any attacking threat.

The Icelandic international is excited about returning to the Premiership where he feels that he has not really proved himself.

Gerry Taggart

Defender

Place of Birth	Belfast, Northern Ireland
Height	1.85m
Date of Birth	18/10/70
Weight	88kg

When Bolton had their first shot at the Premiership in the 95/96 season they felt that with their record signing of £1.5 million, Gerry Taggart, would have helped them in their struggle to stay up. Unfortunately he was injured for the majority of the season but his return in the promotion winning season certainly played a major factor in Bolton's romp to the title.

The Northern Ireland defender will certainly be given a chance to prove himself in the top flight; with defence being manager Colin Todd's major area of concern, Gerry can be sure his place will not be under threat.

Player to Watch

Nathan Blake

Striker

Place of Birth	Cardiff, Wales
Height	1.80m
Date of Birth	27/01/72
Weight	89kg

Nathan has always been regarded as a top marksman but unfortunately he's been bought to help clubs survive in the top division and each time the club has been relegated: first with Sheffield United and then with Bolton.

But he proved in the 96/97 season that he had the character to come back from the disappointment of being relegated again with some cracking performances, scoring over 20 goals.

Yet while there may be strikers bought to try to help Bolton stay up, it is felt by many that Nathan now has the experience to know what it takes to play in the Premiership and will fight for his place.

Bolton Wanderers

Per Frandsen

Midfielder

Place of Birth Dinamarca, Denmark

Height 1.81m

Date of Birth 06/02/70

Weight 79kg

When brought over from Lille at the beginning of the 96/97 campaign Bolton fans were disappointed with the lack of big name signings. After suffering relegation, they were hoping for some big names. Yet Per made a name for himself at Burnden Park and many are saying that he can go on to follow in the footsteps of another great Dane who made it in English football, Jan Molby.

He is a midfielder with great distribution and his range of passing is quite extraordinary. I am sure the Bolton fans are in two minds over what they want from him; if he performs to his capabilities then he is likely to get snapped up by a bigger club.

Player of the Season

John McGinlay

Striker

Place of Birth Inverness, Scotland

Height 1.87m

Date of Birth 08/04/64

Weight 79kg

When Bolton were relegated in 95/96 it was felt that of all the relegated teams they had the least chance of returning to the Premiership. They were thought to have a stale strikeforce, who were unable to find the net on a regular basis – how wrong the critics were.

At 33, John was the leading marksman in the First Division and showed the rest of the country that he was still one of the best finishers in the Football League.

Having hit the net over 30 times he was the main reason why Bolton's runaway success was so great; the team seemed to thrive on John's confidence and golden goalscoring touch. Last season also saw John being looked at once more by Craig Brown for the Scottish national side.

Scott Sellars

Midfielder

Place of Birth Sheffield, England

Height 1.75m

Date of Birth 27/11/65

Weight 65kg

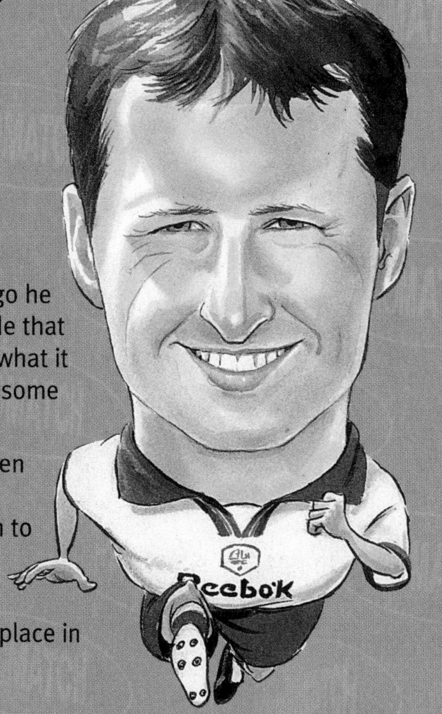

When signed from Newcastle a couple of seasons ago he was by far the most talented player in the Bolton side that was relegated. He has since shown that he still has what it takes to battle his way up into the Premiership with some sterling performances in the 96/97 campaign.

The former Leeds and Blackburn man has always been thought of as one of the most skillful players in the game but has never really had the fight and strength to match. Yet in the past season he has shown that with experience comes strength.

He will play a crucial part if Bolton are to keep their place in the Premiership in the coming season.

Bolton Wanderers

STATS & FACTS

Club Details

Manager: Colin Todd

Captain: Gudni Berggson

Colours: Home - White and Blue

Away - Navy Blue and Blue

Ground: Reebok Stadium

Capacity: 25,000

CLUB HONOURS

FA Cup
Winners - 1923, 1926, 1929, 1958

What are their chances?

Can they stay up? That is the question that everyone will ask themselves. If they look at what Leicester City achieved on their return to the top flight after a year out there is no reason why Bolton cannot fight off the thought of relegation.

Though there is the necessary fight there and experience of life in the Premiership, what it comes down to is that three teams must go down and those with the least quality seem set to drop. To survive, Bolton must buy otherwise they look like a good bet to go straight back down again.

Bolton won't want to become one of those yo-yo clubs; too good for the First Division, not good enough for the Premiership.

PAST RECORD

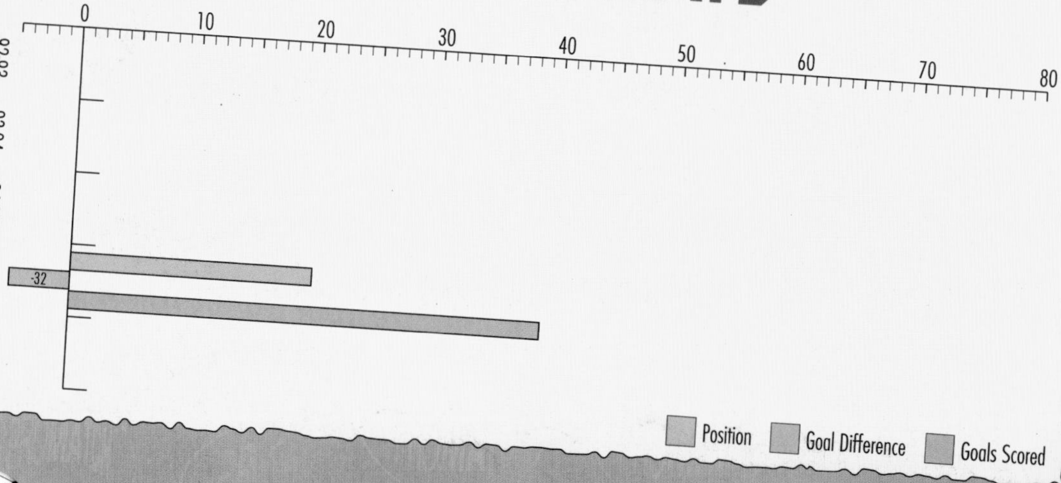

TITLE ODDS

250/1

ON AUGUST 9TH START OF SEASON

Bolton Wanderers

TEAM POSITIONS AND LINE-UP

1 KEITH BRANAGAN	2 GUDNI BERGSSON	3 JIMMY PHILLIPS	4 GERRY TAGGART	5 CHRIS FAIRCLOUGH	6 PER FRANDSEN
7 DAVID LEE	8 ALAN THOMPSON	9 NATHAN BLAKE	10 JOHN MCGINLAY	11 SCOTT SELLARS	12 BRYAN SMALL
13 GAVIN WARD	14 SCOTT GREEN	15 SIMON COLEMAN	16 MICHAEL JOHANSEN	17 STEVE MCANESPIE	18 MIXU PAATELAINEN
19 ANDY TODD	20 JAMIE POLLOCK	21 NEIL COX	22	23	24
25	26	27	28	29	30
31	32	33	34	35	36

Frank Leboeuf

Defender

Place of Birth	Marseille, France
Height	1.84m
Date of Birth	22/01/68
Weight	76kg

Many foreign central defenders exude an air of quality and confidence; Bilic and Albert among them. Frank definitely fits into this category and there is no doubt that he deserves his Stamford Bridge hero status.

When purchased for £2.5 million many fans knew little about the 29 year-old Frenchman but he easily slotted into the pace of the English game and quickly made a name for himself as a really tough customer.

He showed opposing strikers that he really is not someone they should mess with. Opposing goalkeepers are also wary of Frank as he has one of the most powerful shots in the Premiership and was amongst Chelsea's top scorers.

It was his penalty which controversially knocked Leicester out of the FA Cup last season.

Eddie Newton

Midfielder

Place of Birth	Hammersmith, England
Height	1.80m
Date of Birth	13/12/71
Weight	77kg

Much criticism in the past has been directed at the lack of a tough tackling Chelsea midfielder to win the ball but in the 96/97 campaign we saw Eddie take his chance. In doing so, he probably saved Ruud several million pounds.

A likeable character, Eddie has grown up through the Chelsea ranks and has always been vying for a regular place. If he can keep clear of injury that holding role in the middle of the park is his.

He still lacks the international class of some of his Stamford Bridge colleagues but he's a hard working player who gives 100% commitment the whole time and this is why he is so liked by the Stamford Bridge faithful. They like him even more after his clinching goal in the Cup Final.

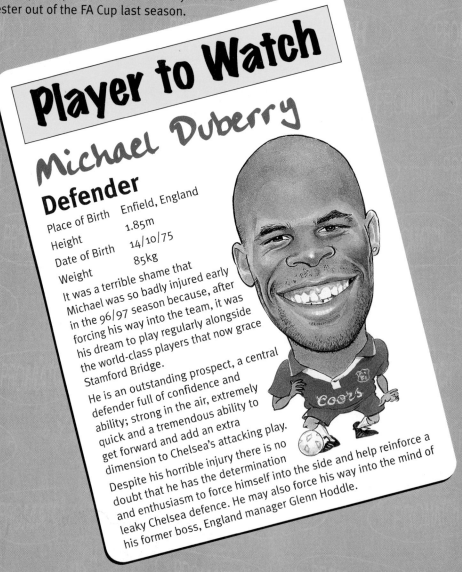

Player to Watch

Michael Duberry

Defender

Place of Birth	Enfield, England
Height	1.85m
Date of Birth	14/10/75
Weight	85kg

It was a terrible shame that Michael was so badly injured early in the 96/97 season because, after forcing his way into the team, it was his dream to play regularly alongside the world-class players that now grace Stamford Bridge.

He is an outstanding prospect, a central defender full of confidence and ability; strong in the air, extremely quick and a tremendous ability to get forward and add an extra dimension to Chelsea's attacking play.

Despite his horrible injury there is no doubt that he has the determination and enthusiasm to force himself into the side and help reinforce a leaky Chelsea defence. He may also force his way into the mind of his former boss, England manager Glenn Hoddle.

Chelsea

Player of the Season

Gianfranco Zola

Striker

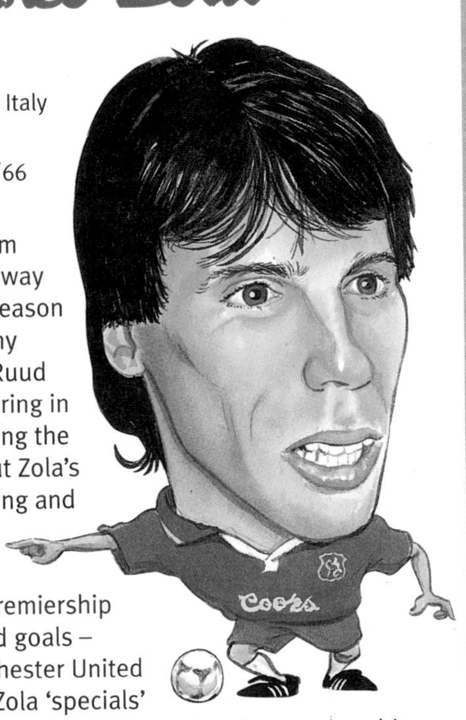

Place of Birth	Oliena, Italy
Height	1.70m
Date of Birth	05/07/66
Weight	70kg

When purchased from Parma a third of the way through the 96/97 season for £4.5 million, many people questioned Ruud Gullit's decision to bring in another Italian nearing the end of his career. But Zola's football did the talking and answered the critics for him.

He brought to the Premiership magnificent skill and goals – Liverpool and Manchester United both suffered from Zola 'specials' last season. The free role Gullit gives Gianfranco gives him a licence to create havoc.

He reached a double figure goal total, which is a fair tally considering he doesn't play in a direct striker's position. There's no doubt that he will play a crucial role as the Chelsea bandwagon gathers momentum.

Mark Hughes

Striker

Place of Birth	Wrexham, Wales
Height	1.75m
Date of Birth	01/11/63
Weight	75kg

With the arrival of Gianluca Vialli and Gianfranco Zola it looked as though the Italian connection would see the end of Mark Hughes' brief time at Chelsea. But most knew that 'Sparky' would not give up trying to force his way into Ruud Gullit's plans, and he did so with some tremendous performances, leaving Vialli frustrated on the sidelines.

A typical British striker with a rugged attitude, he uses strength and power to compensate for a lack of pace; many defenders say that Hughes is probably the most difficult striker to play against.

It'd be a brave person who'd write off Mark playing a major role in Chelsea's 97/98 challenge. His mere presence turned the game in the second half of Chelsea's epic FA Cup win over Liverpool last season.

Roberto Di Matteo

Midfielder

Place of Birth	Schaffhausen, Switzerland
Height	1.79m
Date of Birth	13/01/70
Weight	75kg

When snapped up for £4.9 million in the summer of 96 there were those who envied Chelsea having the little Italian and those who thought that it was a huge risk. Now everyone envies Chelsea.

He had a glorious first year in the Premiership looking as though he really has enjoyed the football. His fantastic FA Cup Final goal was merely the icing on the cake.

Ex-team mate Paul Gascoigne had this to say about Roberto: 'When he was at Lazio he was a quiet youngster who always looked as though he had the potential but now he is stronger, fitter and scoring goals and is one of the best buys in the Premiership.'

Chelsea

STATS & FACTS

Club Details

Manager: Ruud Gullit

Assistant Manager: Graham Rix

Captain: Dennis Wise

Colours: Home - Blue and White

Away - Yellow and Sky

Ground: Stamford Bridge

Capacity: 41,000

CLUB HONOURS

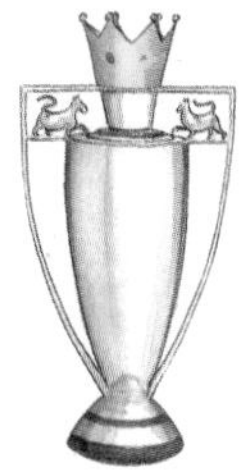

League
Champions - 1954-55

FA Cup
Winners - 1970, 1997

League Cup
Winners - 1965

European Cup Winners Cup
Winners - 1971

What are their chances?

Even though Chelsea are still inconsistent, Ruud is starting to put his masterplan together and the rebuilding process at Chelsea has begun. Gullit's ambition when he took over was to make Chelsea great again and it looks as though he's going the right way about it. The FA Cup was a good start.

With players like Zola, Leboeuf, Duberry and Di Matteo, Chelsea are taking shape as a world class side. With the arrival of more superstars imminent it's felt that in the coming season Chelsea can mount a serious bid for the title.

PAST RECORD

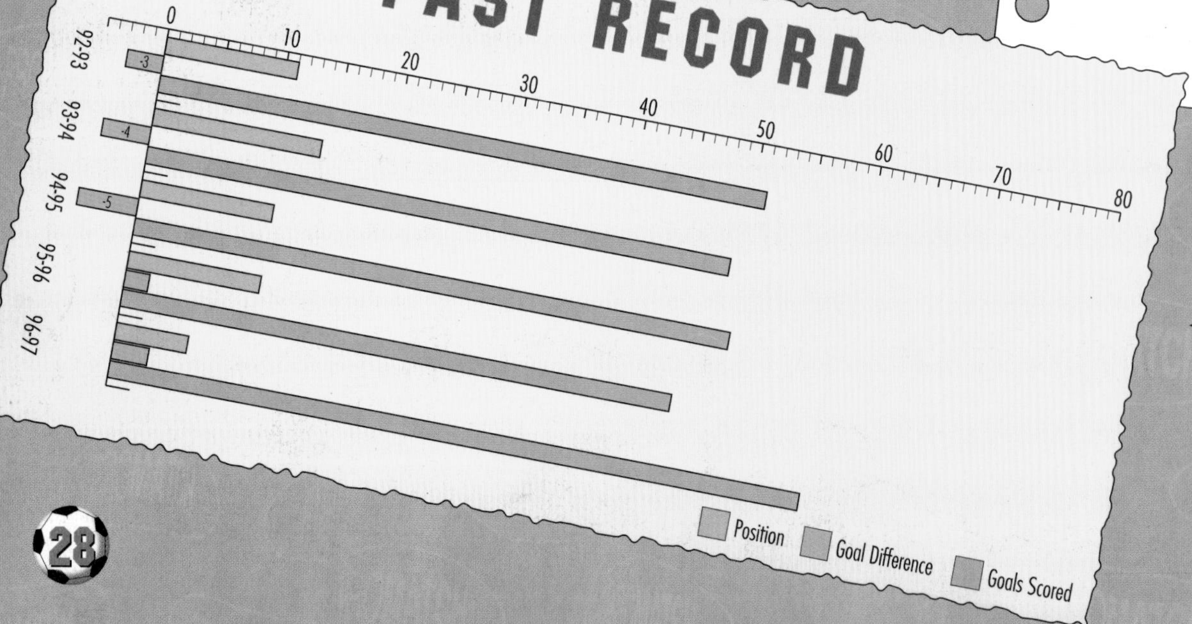

TITLE ODDS

10/1

ON AUGUST 9TH START OF SEASON

Chelsea

TEAM POSITIONS AND LINE-UP

1 DMITRI KHARINE	2 DAN PETRESCU	3 CELESTINE BABAYARO	4 RUUD GULLIT	5 FRANK LEBOEUF	6 STEVE CLARKE
7 EDDIE NEWTON	8 ANDY MYERS	9 GIANLUCA VIALLI	10 MARK HUGHES	11 DENNIS WISE	12 MICHAEL DUBERRY
13 KEVIN HITCHCOCK	14 CRAIG BURLEY	15 DAVID LEE	16 ROBERTO DI MATTEO	17 SCOTT MINTO	18 GUSTAVO POYET
19	20 FRANK SINCLAIR	21 JODY MORRIS	22 MARK NICHOLLS	23	24
25 GIANFRANCO ZOLA	26	27	28	29	30
31	32	33	34	35	36

Dion Dublin

Striker

Place of Birth	Leicester, England
Height	1.83m
Date of Birth	22/04/69
Weight	80kg

Faced with another relegation battle Dion once more proved invaluable to the Coventry City side, whether in defence or in attack he showed true grit and determination, inspiring confidence throughout the team.

In a season that saw Dion proving that he has the qualities to play at the back, as well as lead the attack, he scored fewer goals than normal.

He will go into the next season hoping that he can take Coventry to a cup final or even a place in Europe.

John Salako

Midfielder

Place of Birth	Nigeria
Height	1.75m
Date of Birth	11/02/69
Weight	70kg

Despite having to sit out the final third of the season through injury, John showed that he is still one of the most effective wingers in England with a touch of Brazilian flair to his game.

It is no surprise that during the 96/97 season it was John's injury that coincided with Coventry's slump in form and it really does prove that he is one of the Sky Blues most valuable players.

When he has once again recovered full fitness he will have to regain the form that could force him back into the international limelight.

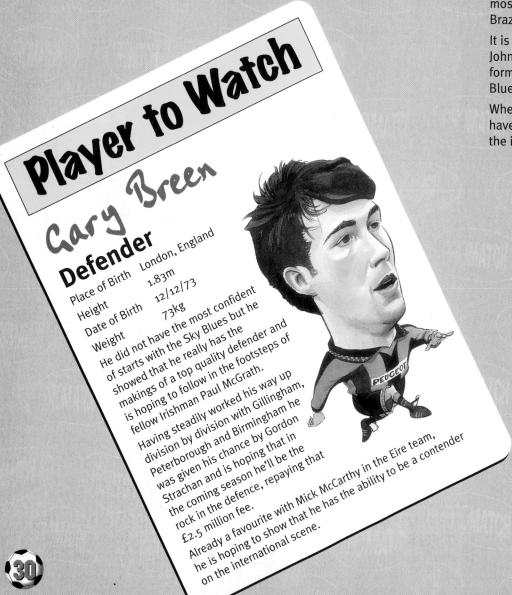

Player to Watch

Gary Breen

Defender

Place of Birth	London, England
Height	1.83m
Date of Birth	12/12/73
Weight	73kg

He did not have the most confident of starts with the Sky Blues but he showed that he really has the makings of a top quality defender and is hoping to follow in the footsteps of fellow Irishman Paul McGrath.

Having steadily worked his way up division by division with Gillingham, Peterborough and Birmingham he was given his chance by Gordon Strachan and is hoping that in the coming season he'll be the rock in the defence, repaying that £2.5 million fee.

Already a favourite with Mick McCarthy in the Eire team, he is hoping to show that he has the ability to be a contender on the international scene.

Gary McAllister

Midfielder

Place of Birth Motherwell, Scotland

Height 1.86m

Date of Birth 25/12/64

Weight 68kg

He astounded everyone in the English game by switching to Coventry from Leeds in a £3 million deal especially as City nearly always struggle against relegation. Even though they narrowly avoided the drop, Gary managed to show those who doubted the wisdom of his move that he has joined a club with ambition and promise.

The inspirational midfielder has again proved that he is one of the most talented players in the game. He has an eye for a pass that means he can measure the ball to any part of the pitch.

He looks forward to another season with Coventry along with the added attraction of trying to help Scotland into the World Cup Finals in 98.

Player of the Season

Darren Huckerby

Striker

Place of Birth Nottingham, England

Height 1.80m

Date of Birth 23/04/76

Weight 71kg

When purchased from Newcastle for just over £1 million, many were quick to criticise the judgement of Gordon Strachan once more, yet even Gordon is surprised how easily Darren has defied such critics.

His lightning speed and awesome presence in and around the penalty area are the major reasons why Coventry stayed in the Premiership.

At only 21 years of age he is one of England's brightest prospects and, having already been noticed at Under-21 level, there is no doubt that he will go on to play a major role for England in the future.

Coventry

Noel Whelan

Striker

Place of Birth Leeds, England

Height 1.80m

Date of Birth 30/12/74

Weight 73kg

When Noel arrived from Leeds in the 95/96 season he had a similar impact to that of his team mate Darren Huckerby in 96/97. Both set the Premiership alight with some devastating performances.

Though the 96/97 season has not proved as successful as the season before, Noel has still shown that he is a player of much ability and is a striker that defences should not take lightly.

At only 23 he has much ahead of him and the Coventry faithful will be hoping that he will be able to form a prolific partnership with Huckerby.

Coventry

STATS & FACTS

Club Details

Manager: Gordon Strachan

Assistant Manager: Gary Pendrey

Captain: Dion Dublin

Colours: Home - Dark Blue and Sky Blue

Away - Red and Navy

Ground: Highfield Road

Capacity: 23,500

CLUB HONOURS

FA Cup
Winners - 1987

What are their chances?

After such hopes and aspirations for last season, only to endure a season of struggle, they will be desperate not to have a repeat performance.

With the squad that has been bought by Strachan and his predecessor, they are definitely capable of achieving a mid-table place and would be a good outside bet for a cup.

PAST RECORD

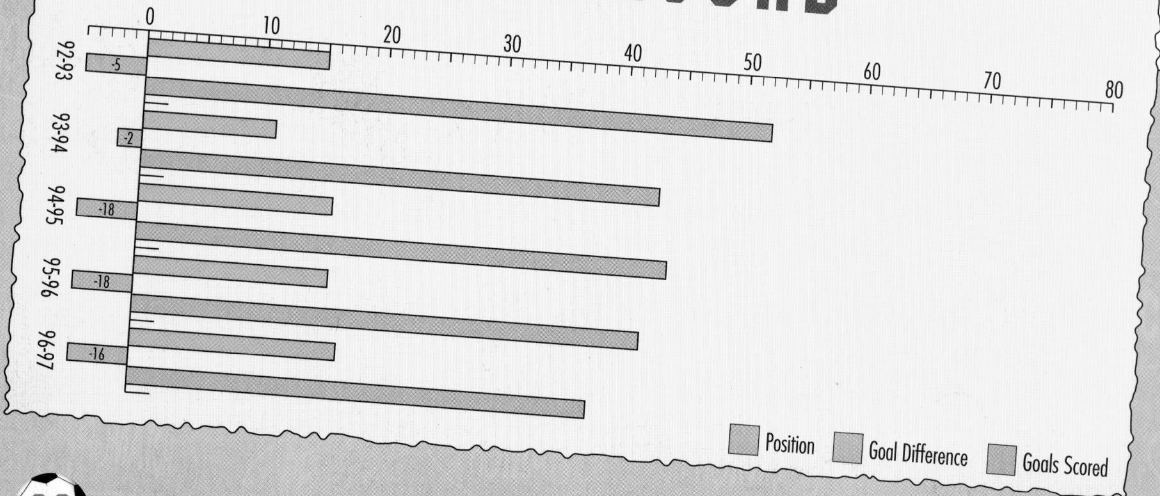

TITLE ODDS

200/1

ON AUGUST 9TH START OF SEASON

Coventry

TEAM POSITIONS AND LINE-UP

1 STEVE ORGRIZOVIC	2 RICHARD SHAW	3 DAVID BURROWS	4 PAUL WILLIAMS	5 LIAM DAISH	6 KEVIN RICHARDSON
7 EOIN JESS	8 NOEL WHELAN	9 DION DUBLIN	10 GARY MCALLISTER	11 JOHN SALAKO	12 PAUL TELFER
13 JOHN FILAN	14 PETER NDLOVU	15 MARQUES ISRAS	16 BRIAN BORROWS	17 WILLIE BOLAND	18 MARCUS HALL
19	20 MICHAEL O'NEILL	21 ANDREW DUCROS	22	23	24
25 GARY BREEN	26 GORDON STRACHAN	27	28 DARREN HUCKERBY	29	30
31	32	33	34	35	36

David Hopkin

Midfielder

Place of Birth	Greenock, Scotland
Height	1.77m
Date of Birth	21/08/70
Weight	75kg

Another very influential Palace player who can't wait to show the Chelsea staff that he should have never been allowed to leave Stamford Bridge.

The Scottish attacking midfielder has revelled in the First Division since his arrival at Palace and he's hoping that his form can continue to be as impressive when he gets the chance to play in the Premiership.

On occasions he's been inconsistent but generally he has proved to be a bargain for the price that Palace paid for him. With the Scottish team desperate to try and find a player who can score goals from midfield, David is perfect to fill this role. Craig Brown will no doubt see more of David now he's playing in the higher profile Premiership.

Ray Houghton

Midfielder

Place of Birth	Glasgow, Scotland
Height	1.74m
Date of Birth	09/01/62
Weight	72kg

One of the great pros in the English league, the Republic of Ireland midfielder is still proving that he is one of the top all-round midfielders playing in the English game.

Having had plenty of Premiership experience with Aston Villa and Liverpool, Ray will play a major part in trying to help Steve Coppell and his side achieve their ultimate goal in the coming season - Premiership survival.

Approaching his 36th birthday he's had an astonishing career yet still manages to find the energy to put 100% into every game that he plays – a great player.

Player to Watch

Andy Roberts

Midfielder

Place of Birth	Dartford, England
Height	1.78m
Date of Birth	20/03/74
Weight	82kg

Bought from Millwall, in a multi-million pound deal a couple of seasons ago, he has been one of the most outstanding players in the Football League over the past two years.

Able to play in the centre of defence or midfield, he has a great range of passing and his tackling is nearly always timed to perfection.

Although he does not get on the scoresheet as much as he would like, Andy's potential has been noted by many top clubs in the Premiership but Steve Coppell is desperate to keep hold of him and sees him as a vital part of Palace's resurgence.

Crystal Palace

Dean Gordon

Defender

Place of Birth Thornton Heath, England
Height 1.80m
Date of Birth 10/02/73
Weight 82kg

Forever being linked with some of the top clubs in England, Dean is just happy that he has helped his team into the Premiership again where he will try and fulfil his ambition of helping Palace gain top flight respectability.

The pacey left-back has all the qualities a full-back should have – speed, timing, tackling; he also packs a powerful shot that has proved a matchwinner on many occasions.

Having gained Under-21 caps in the past for England, he is hoping that he can now turn them into full caps.

Player of the Season

Bruce Dyer

Striker

Place of Birth Ilford, England
Height 1.78m
Date of Birth 13/04/75
Weight 70kg

Breaking the transfer record by becoming the youngest player to be bought in a million pound deal, it seemed that the pressure got to Bruce and he didn't find the net with the same regularity as he did in his Watford days.

Yet in the 96/97 campaign he finally won over the Selhurst Park faithful with some spectacular performances and wonderful goals.

He is at his most dangerous when he has the ball at his feet and he's running at defenders. At only 22 he has ambitions to try and get into the England side and now has the chance of impressing Glenn Hoddle in the Premiership.

Dougie Freedman

Striker

Place of Birth Glasgow, Scotland
Height 1.78m
Date of Birth 21/01/74
Weight 74kg

Not always a first team regular he is still a favourite with the fans and has the ability to go on to prove a real success in the top flight.

Having scored some vital goals for Palace in the 96/97 campaign, especially in the playoffs, he was still sometimes thought of being too rash and eccentric to play in the rough and ready First Division.

Having started his career with QPR before moving to Barnet, where he scored over a goal every two games, he is on the way up and it would be no surprise to see a top club come in for the promising Scotsman.

Crystal Palace

STATS & FACTS

Club Details

Manager: Steve Coppell

Assistant Manager: Ray Lewington

Captain: Andy Roberts

Colours: Home - Blue and Red
Away - White and Blue

Ground: Selhurst Park

Capacity: 26,400

What are their chances?

After creeping into the playoffs at the last gasp and then surging through into the Premiership, Steve Coppell has done a magnificent job second time around. Yet he is going to have to work miracles to try and keep Palace in the top flight.

There are many talented players in the squad but there are very few with Premiership experience and this will prove a major obstacle.

If Coppell brings in some older heads and tries to keep hold of players such as Roberts, Dyer and Hopkin then they have a chance.

PAST RECORD

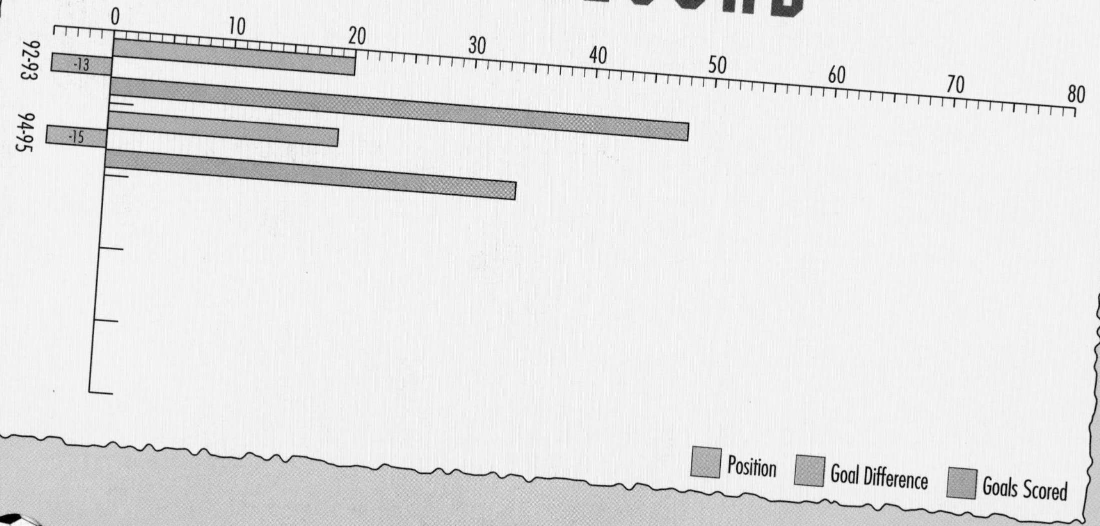

TITLE ODDS

250/1

ON AUGUST 9TH START OF SEASON

Crystal Palace

TEAM POSITIONS AND LINE-UP

1	CHRIS DAY
2	MARCUS EDWORTHY
3	DEAN GORDON
4	KEVIN MUSCAT
5	ANDY ROBERTS
6	DAVID TUTTLE
7	DAVID HOPKIN
8	RAY HOUGHTON
9	DOUGIE FREEDMAN
10	NEIL SHIPPERLEY
11	BRUCE DYER
12	CARL VEART
13	ROBERT QUINN
14	GEORGE NDAH
15	LEON MCKENZIE
16	LEIT ANDERSON
17	DARREN PITCHER
18	SIMON RODGER
19	GARETH DAVIES
20	GARETH BOXELL
21	CARLO NASH
22	
23	
24	
25	
26	
27	
28	
29	
30	
31	
32	
33	
34	
35	
36	

Chris Powell

Defender

Place of Birth Lambeth, England
Height 1.78m
Date of Birth 08/09/69
Weight 73kg

Many doubted that Chris had the ability to play in the Premiership and after being looked at by so many top flight clubs in the past and being considered not good enough, he seems to have proved everyone wrong by becoming one of Derby's most consistent players.

His defending qualities are sometimes suspect but he is one of the most attack-minded full-backs in the Premiership and has proved a handful for many opposing right-backs.

His speed and crossing accuracy have made him one of the first on Jim Smith's team sheet and it is easy to see the pleasure Chris gets out of being able to prove all of his doubters wrong.

Igor Stimac

Defender

Place of Birth Split, Croatia
Height 1.86m
Date of Birth 06/09/67
Weight 76kg

Before Derby made it to the Premiership Igor was talked about as being the best defender outside the Premiership, and he has not let himself down by putting in some gritty performances.

Despite suffering for much of the season with niggling injuries, when he played for Derby the difference in their defence was outstanding.The leakage of silly goals was much less frequent when Igor was playing.

Along with fellow countryman Asanovic, he started his career with Hadjuk Split and then saw his reputation grow throughout Europe. A bid from one of the top clubs in Spain looks to have been rejected as Jim Smith sees Igor as a major part in his rebuilding of Derby County.

Player to Watch

Christian Dailly

Midfielder

Place of Birth Dundee, Scotland
Height 1.78m
Date of Birth 23/10/73
Weight 68kg

When first arriving in the summer of 96 from Dundee United, very little was known about the Scottish midfielder except that he had turned down a lucrative deal to Manchester City days before his move to Derby.

He played a part in Derby's 96/97 season but was rested on occasions and also picked up some minor injuries.

Many have said that he is the complete midfielder and have likened him to Graeme Souness, with that same bite and vision in his play.

Dean Sturridge

Striker

Place of Birth Birmingham, England
Height 1.73m
Date of Birth 27/07/73
Weight 77kg

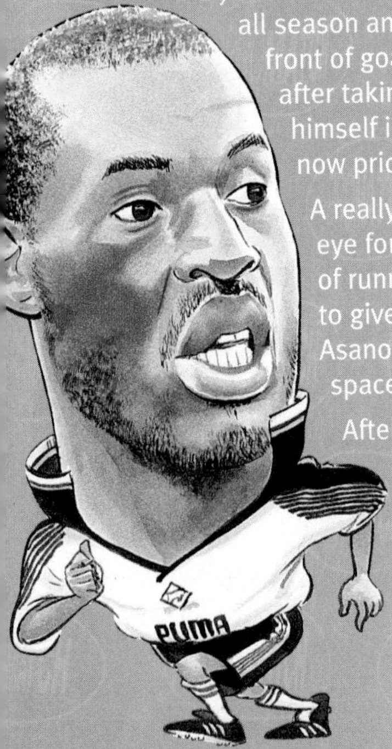

Dynamite Dean has devastated defences all season and has been so deadly in front of goal! Seriously though, after taking a while to register himself in the Derby side Dean is now priceless to the club.

A really fast player who has an eye for goal and also does a lot of running off the ball in order to give players such as Asanovic and Van der Laan space to manoeuvre.

After a great start to the 96/97 season, the goals dried up but he can be happy with what he has achieved in his first season in the Premiership.

Player of the Season

Alijosa Asanovic

Midfielder

Place of Birth Split, Croatia
Height 1.86m
Date of Birth 14/12/65
Weight 76kg

After impressing so many playing for Croatia in the European Championships, he carried on the rich vein of form right throughout the 96/97 season and played a major part in helping The Rams survive in the top flight.

Arguably one of the most talented players to grace the English game his attitude has not always been 100% and that has brought criticism, yet he defies his critics on many an occasion by letting his football do the talking.

Whether the midfielder remains at Derby is touch-and-go, yet he will always be remembered for some of the most wonderful performances ever seen at the Baseball Ground.

Derby County

Robin Van der Laan

Midfielder

Place of Birth Scheidam, The Netherlands
Height 1.80m
Date of Birth 05/09/68
Weight 78kg

After taking Derby into the Premiership as captain in the 95/96 campaign he found himself out of favour and was put out on loan to a few First Division sides; it was felt that Robin did not really have what it takes for the top flight, yet he proved everyone wrong when recalled and was a regular in the last third of the season.

A skillful player who also has the steel to match his silky skills though he has been accused on occasions of laziness, but since his return to the side he has made extra efforts with his fitness and there has been no sign of any lacklustre performances.

The former Port Vale man is not one of the most sprightly players in the line-up yet hopes to be fighting for his place at Derby next season.

Derby County

STATS & FACTS

Club Details

Manager: Jim Smith

Assistant Manager: Steve McClaren

Captain: Igor Stimac

Colours: Home - White and Black
Away - Maroon and White

Ground: Pride Park

Capacity: 30,000

CLUB HONOURS

League
Champions - 1971-72, 1974-75

FA Cup
Winners - 1946

What are their chances?

Derby were strongly tipped to be relegated before the start of their first season in the Premiership and although they stayed up, if new faces are not brought in, especially at the back, then it could be a hard season for Jim Smith and his men.

There are quality players there with Sturridge, Asanovic and the new Costa Rican, Wanchope, yet if the squad is not added to then it looks like they could again be dropping from the top flight.

PAST RECORD

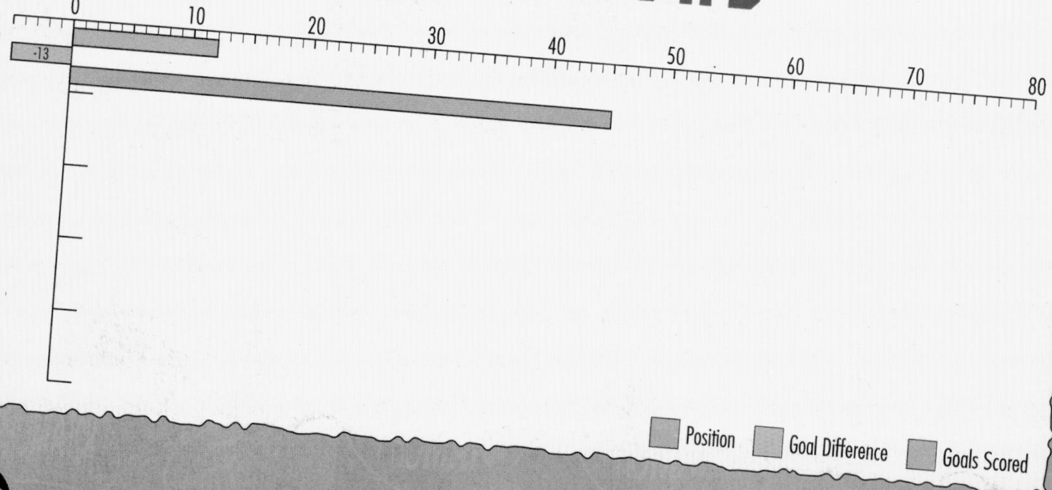

TITLE ODDS
150/1
ON AUGUST 9TH START OF SEASON

Derby County

TEAM POSITIONS AND LINE-UP

1 RUSSELL HOULT	2 GARY ROWETT	3 CHRIS POWELL	4 DARYLL POWELL	5 DEAN YATES	6 IGOR STIMAC
7 ROBIN VAN DER LAAN	8 DEAN STURRIDGE	9 MARCO GABBIADINI	10 ALIJOSA ASANOVIC	11 RON WILLEMS	12 ASHLEY WARD
13 MARTIN TAYLOR	14 PAUL SIMPSON	15 PAUL TROLLOPE	16 JACOB LAURSEN	17 MATT CARBON	18 LEE CARSLEY
19 SEAN FLYNN	20	21	22 CHRISTIAN DAILLY	23	24
25	26	27 PAUL MCGRATH	28 MART POOM	29 PAULO WANCHOPE	30
31	32	33	34	35	36

Duncan Ferguson

Striker

Place of Birth	Stirling, Scotland
Height	1.90m
Date of Birth	27/12/71
Weight	84kg

The 96/97 season did not prove to be so successful as his others for the Toffees, yet he still proved to be a real threat for opposing teams and their defences.

A player with enormous potential who is beginning to calm his suspect temperament, yet he was still out for quite long spells of the season, suffering from niggling injuries.

He is hoping to make his place in the Scottish line-up a permanent fixture and, along with Kevin Gallacher, he forms a deadly partnership, mixing strength and skill.

Nicky Barmby

Striker

Place of Birth	Hull, England
Height	1.68m
Date of Birth	12/02/74
Weight	72kg

Many were surprised when Bryan Robson was willing to let a player as talented as Nicky leave, but what was Middlesbrough's loss is most definitely Everton's gain.

Even since his Spurs days he has been thought of as one the Premiership's hottest properties and Nicky's been a regular at both club and international level.

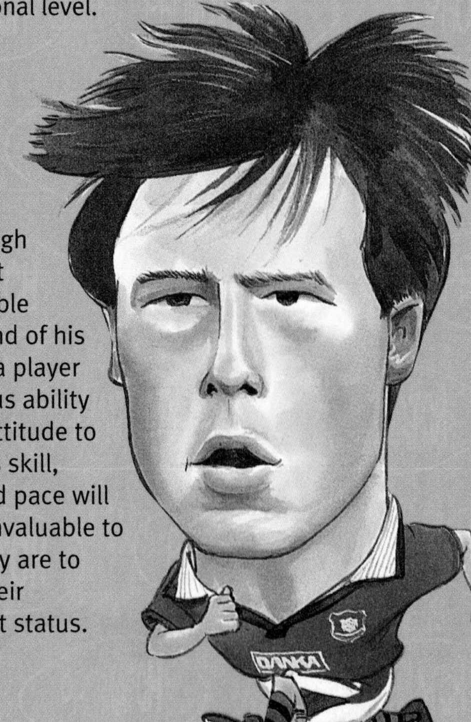

At only 23 he has commanded transfer fees of over £10 million and it looks as though he will almost certainly double that by the end of his career. He is a player with enormous ability and a good attitude to the game; his skill, versatility and pace will prove to be invaluable to Everton if they are to wake from their sleeping giant status.

Player to Watch

Michael Branch

Striker

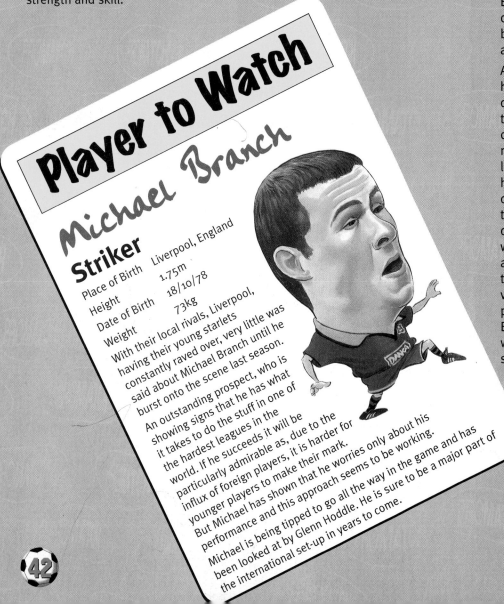

Place of Birth	Liverpool, England
Height	1.75m
Date of Birth	18/10/78
Weight	73kg

With their local rivals, Liverpool, having their young starlets constantly raved over, very little was said about Michael Branch until he burst onto the scene last season.

An outstanding prospect, who is showing signs that he has what it takes to do the stuff in one of the hardest leagues in the world. If he succeeds it will be particularly admirable as, due to the influx of foreign players, it is harder for younger players to make their mark. But Michael has shown that he worries only about his performance and this approach seems to be working. Michael is being tipped to go all the way in the game and has been looked at by Glenn Hoddle. He is sure to be a major part of the international set-up in years to come.

Slaven Bilic

Defender

Place of Birth	Croatia
Height	1.85m
Date of Birth	11/09/68
Weight	85kg

Arriving at West Ham a couple of seasons ago few had heard of the Croatian centre-half. Yet he has now proved himself as one of the most accomplished defenders in European football.

Having become a cult hero at Upton Park, he opted for a big money move to Everton and was made the highest paid defender in England. His £4.5 million move will not adversely affect his game as he has proven that he can cope with pressure, having played for a struggling, relegation threatened team.

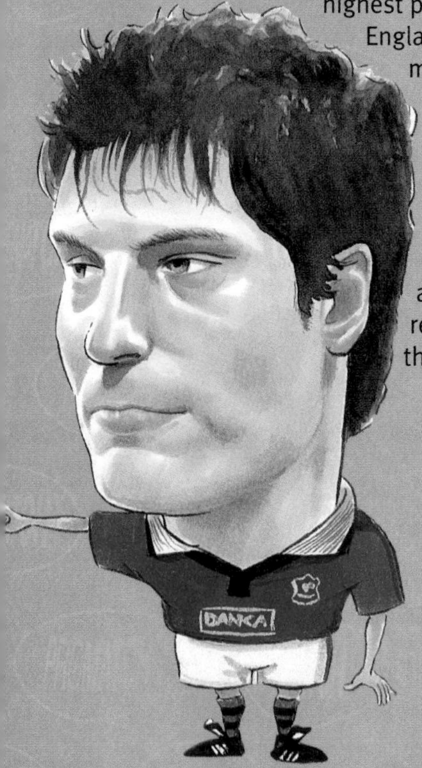

Player of the Season

Gary Speed

Midfielder

Place of Birth	Hawarden, Wales
Height	1.75m
Date of Birth	08/09/69
Weight	66kg

When signed from Leeds for £3.5 million it was felt that it was a good move all round, enabling Gary to further his career by trying his luck at a different club. Everton fitted the bill having just enjoyed a season which suggested their future looked bright.

Even though the season for Everton did not go to plan, Gary certainly made an impact at Goodison Park and he showed that a big money move did not alter how much effort he was going to put into his game.

Now at the peak of his career, the Welsh international's performances were the highlight of Everton's poor season.

Earl Barrett

Defender

Place of Birth	Rochdale, England
Height	1.80m
Date of Birth	28/04/67
Weight	70kg

Having made the highest amount of appearances for Everton in one of their most dismal seasons in the Premiership, he was also probably the most consistent player in the side.

He looked to have regained the form that forced him into the England squad a couple of years ago and Glenn Hoddle could do a lot worse if he's looking for defensive cover.

At 30 he still has the speed and tenacity that earned him rave reviews in his Villa and Oldham days, and he now seems to have won over his critics in the stands.

Everton

STATS & FACTS

Club Details

Manager: Andy Gray

Assistant Manager: Willie Donachie

Captain: Dave Watson

Colours: Home - White and Blue

Away - Amber and Black

Ground: Goodison Park

Capacity: 40,177

CLUB HONOURS

League
Champions - 1890-91, 1914-15, 1927-28, 1931-32, 1938-39, 1962-63, 1969-70, 1984-85, 1986-87

FA Cup
Winners - 1906, 1933, 1966, 1984, 1995

European Cup Winners Cup
Winners - 1985

What are their chances?

The 95/96 season was one of steady achievement for the Goodison club, leaving their fans anticipating 96/97 with relish. Yet they were bitterly disappointed.

After a promising start, a dip in form saw them in a relegation struggle and Joe Royle lost his job.

Now with a new manager and with new faces at the club there will almost certainly be an improvement, yet I do not see them challenging for the title. They can only hope for a place in Europe.

PAST RECORD

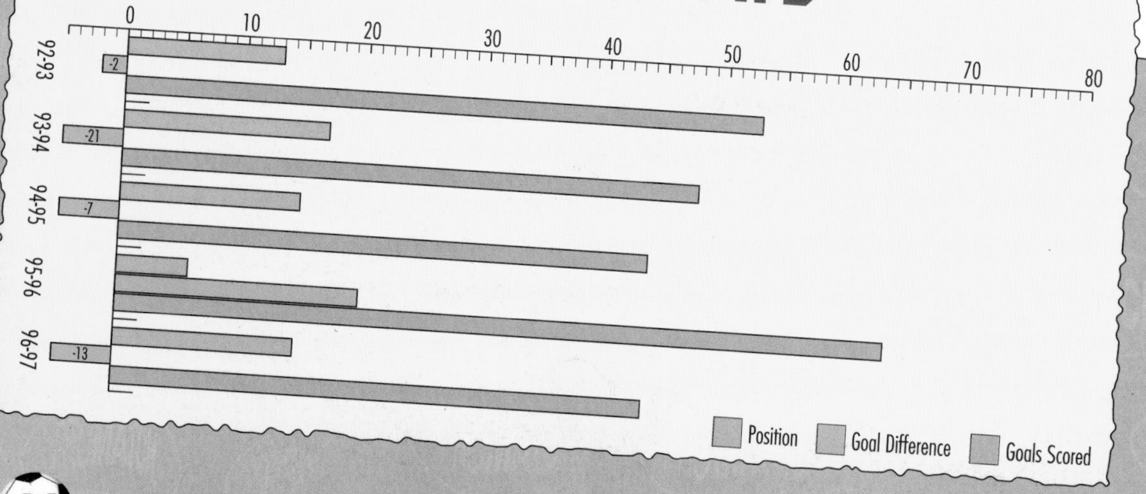

TITLE ODDS

66/1

ON AUGUST 9TH START OF SEASON

Everton

TEAM POSITIONS AND LINE-UP

1	2	3	4	5	6
NEVILLE SOUTHALL	EARL BARRETT	ANDY HINCHCLIFFE	DAVID UNSWORTH	DAVID WATSON	TERRY PHELAN
7	8	9	10	11	12
GRAHAM STUART	PAUL RIDEOUT	DUNCAN FERGUSON	GARY SPEED		NICKY BARMBY
13	14	15	16	17	18
PAUL GERRARD	JOHN EBBRELL	CLAUS THOMSEN	SLAVEN BILIC		JOE PARKINSON
19	20	21	22	23	24
MARC HOTTIGER	TONY GRANT	CRAIG SHORT		MICHAEL BRANCH	
25	26	27	28	29	30
	GRAHAM ALLEN	RICHARD DUNNE			
31	32	33	34	35	36
				JOHN HILLS	

Brian Deane

Striker

Place of Birth	Leeds, England
Height	1.91m
Date of Birth	07/02/68
Weight	79kg

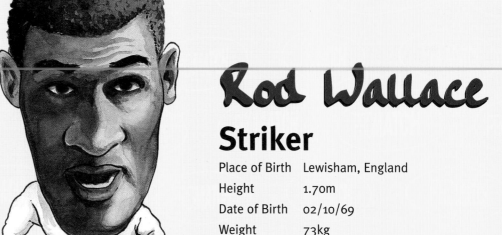

With Tony Yeboah being plagued by injury throughout the 96/97 season, George Graham was tempted to go into the transfer market but the form of Brian Deane was influential in Graham's decision not to use his chequebook.

His time at Leeds has not been a total success yet last season was his best in a Leeds shirt. He adapted to a different role where he played deeper and made more goals than he actually scored.

There has been talk of Brian moving from Elland Road but he has the ability to succeed and, if he can recapture the form of his Sheffield United days, he will do well anywhere, even if it's not at Leeds.

Rod Wallace

Striker

Place of Birth	Lewisham, England
Height	1.70m
Date of Birth	02/10/69
Weight	73kg

Another player who's never really made the expected impact at Leeds; but he was given new confidence under George Graham and finished top scorer for his side in the 96/97 season.

His skills and electric pace have seen a return of the Rodney Wallace that was evident in his Southampton days, and he was one of the real pluses for Leeds in a season when so many others disappointed.

The diminutive striker still has a real talent and the Elland Road faithful just hope that the right players are brought in to play alongside him and that Rodney himself is not on his way out.

Player to Watch

Lee Bowyer

Midfielder

Place of Birth	London, England
Height	1.75m
Date of Birth	03/01/77
Weight	61kg

After his first season in the Premiership he has got applause from all areas, most notably from the England manager Glenn Hoddle. He is one of England's great prospects and is being thought about seriously for an international place.

His terrier-like play, along with some wonderful ability have seen him easily command a first team place. After scoring on his debut, followed by other important goals, he has become quite a hero with the crowd.

In the past, other things have seemed to get in the way of his footballing career but that is all behind him which is quite apparent judging by his performances. He seems a snip at £3 million and is hoping to go on to be one of the Premiership's top players.

Robert Molenaar

Defender

Place of Birth	Votendam, The Netherlands
Height	1.83m
Date of Birth	27/02/69
Weight	82kg

When purchased halfway through the 96/97 season for a cool million pounds it was thought that if George Graham - who knows how to organise a tight defence - bought a defender, he would be one of the highest quality. So it's been proved.

The Dutch bruiser has been quite magnificent since his arrival and seems to fit perfectly into the English game. He is Herculean on the pitch and it is a very rare sight to see him lose out on anything in the air.

Many have remarked on his similarities to Arnold Schwarzenegger and he certainly plays with plenty of fight; one of the bargains of the season.

Player of the Season

Nigel Martyn

Goalkeeper

Place of Birth	St Austell, England
Height	1.88m
Date of Birth	11/08/66
Weight	89kg

During his time with Crystal Palace it was always thought that Nigel was one of the best goalkeepers in the country, but because he played for a less glamorous club he never got the recognition he deserved.

After Palace failed to gain promotion in 95/96, Nigel felt that after being so loyal to the club where he had spent over five seasons, he needed a chance to play at one of the top clubs. George Graham gave Nigel his chance at Leeds.

In his first season with Leeds he was outstanding, and was undoubtedly their player of the year with some outstanding performances and unbelievable saves. He was again looked at by the England coach which reflected how well he had played for his club.

Lee Sharpe

Midfielder

Place of Birth	Halesowen, England
Height	1.80m
Date of Birth	25/05/71
Weight	72kg

His switch from close rivals Manchester United did not really surprise many; Lee is a player with plenty of ambition and he realised that Leeds was a club that could fulfill these ambitions.

He was the first of the wonderkids at Old Trafford but now he has matured a lot and looks like one of the most complete midfielders in the Premiership.

Playing in a more central role, he enjoys getting involved right in the thick of the action whereas at United he was preferred on the wing and was often left out of the side. In his first season for Leeds he has become one of the crowd's favourites and he's hoping to bring some success in the near future to his new club.

Leeds United

STATS & FACTS

Club Details

Manager: George Graham

Assistant Manager: David O'Leary

Captain: Ian Rush

Colours: Home - White, Blue and Yellow

Away - Yellow, White and Blue

Ground: Elland Road

Capacity: 40,000

CLUB HONOURS

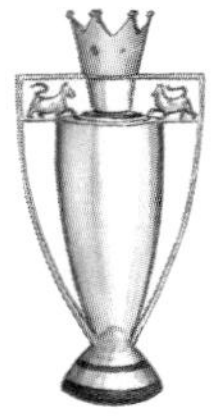

League
Champions - 1968-69, 1973-74, 1991-92

FA Cup
Winners - 1972

League Cup
Winners - 1968

UEFA Cup
Winners - 1968, 1971

What are their chances?

After a mediocre season in the 96/97 campaign George Graham is hoping that with a brand new season he can turn the potential, that so many have talked about, into reality.

With players of the calibre of Bowyer, Sharpe and Martyn and youngsters such as Gray, Harte and Jackson coming through there is much to look forward to and, with the chequebook ready to be used, Leeds could certainly make a few heads turn next year.

PAST RECORD

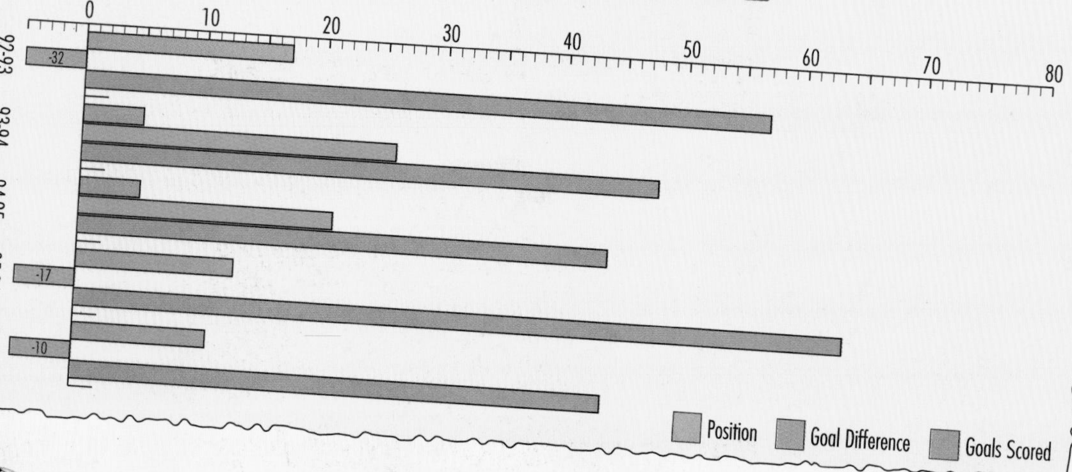

TITLE ODDS
66/1
ON AUGUST 9TH START OF SEASON

Leeds United

TEAM POSITIONS AND LINE-UP

1 NIGEL MARTYN	2 GARY KELLY	3 TONY DORIGO	4 CARLTON PALMER	5 LUCAS RADEBE	6 DAVID WETHERALL
7 LEE SHARPE	8 ROD WALLACE	9 IAN RUSH	10 BRIAN DEANE	11 LEE BOWYER	12 JOHN PEMBERTON
13	14 ANDY GRAY	15 MARK BEENEY	16 RICHARD JOBSON	17 MARK TINKLER	18 GUNNAR HALLE
19 HARRY KEWELL	20 IAN HARTE	21 TONY YEBOAH	22 MARK FORD	23 ANDY COUZENS	24 JASON BLUNT
25 ROBERT BOWMAN	26 PAUL BEESLEY	27 DAVID ROBERTSON	28	29 MARK JACKSON	30 ROBERT MOLENAAR
31	32	33	34 PAUL EVANS	35	36

Neil Lennon

Midfielder

Place of Birth	Lurgan, Northern Ireland
Height	1.75m
Date of Birth	25/06/71
Weight	73kg

Much was said about the young Irishman before the start of the 96/97 season. It was felt that if he could live up to his potential then Leicester would have a chance of staying in the Premiership. He did and they did!

A real battler in the middle of the park, where a lot of his work has gone unnoticed, he has probably been the most consistent player in the side with some absolutely tremendous performances.

The ginger-haired terrier, he has been hailed as the next David Batty and Leicester are going to do all they can to try to hang on to this talent.

Steve Walsh

Defender

Place of Birth	Fulwood, England
Height	1.88m
Date of Birth	03/11/64
Weight	88kg

Captain Marvel is now approaching his testimonial season at Leicester where he is now thought of as part of the club after the devotion and enthusiasm he has shown over the years.

Although not the most cultured of players, he typifies the Leicester way of playing with plenty of hard work and commitment.

With Matt Elliot and Spencer Prior, Steve has formed one of the most solid defences in the Premiership and he hopes that they can repeat last season's feat of going all the way to Wembley.

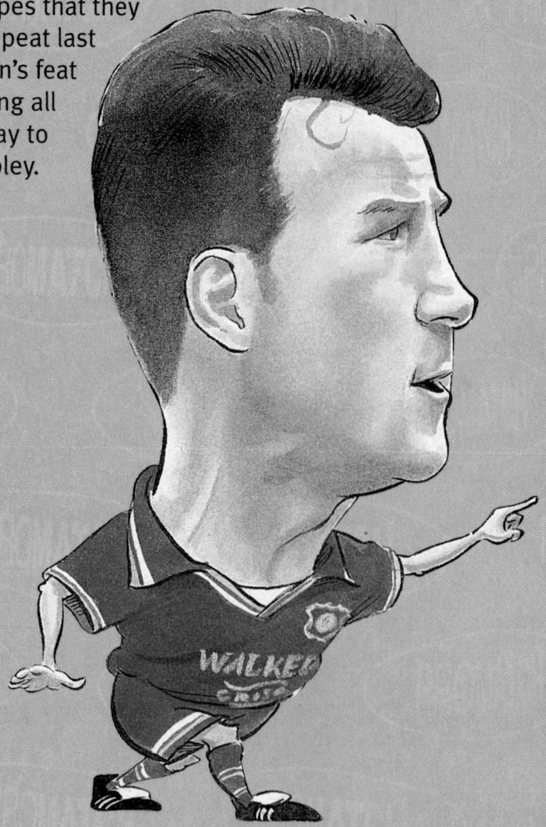

Player to Watch

Emile Heskey

Striker

Place of Birth	Leicester, England
Height	1.88m
Date of Birth	11/01/78
Weight	83kg

Already being put in the £5 million bracket, Emile has surprised many in how comfortably he has slotted into the speed and tenacity of the Premiership game.

'Bruno', as he is nicknamed, had an explosive first season in the Premiership, showing that at only 19 he has more strength on the ball than many strikers in the top flight. Along with his power he has skill and control which makes him a devastating force to play against.

Already tried at England Under-21 level, he is sure to be in Glenn Hoddle's plans for the future as he looks like a forward who can really tear apart defences.

Leicester City

Muzzy Izzett

Midfielder

Place of Birth	London, England
Height	1.78m
Date of Birth	31/10/74
Weight	65kg

Even though Muzzy was never really considered by Glenn Hoddle at Chelsea, Martin O'Neill saw something in the young Londoner that he felt could help his club in the midfield department where they lacked flair.

Muzzy has come in and surprised many with his ability and even though his small frame does not appear to have the strength for the top flight, he is really quite a tough customer and takes a lot of punishment.

At only 22 he is still young and maybe able to force himself onto the international scene. Whatever happens I am sure that he is just happy at being given his chance to play in the top flight.

Player of the Season

Steve Claridge

Striker

Place of Birth	Portsmouth, England
Height	1.81m
Date of Birth	10/04/66
Weight	81kg

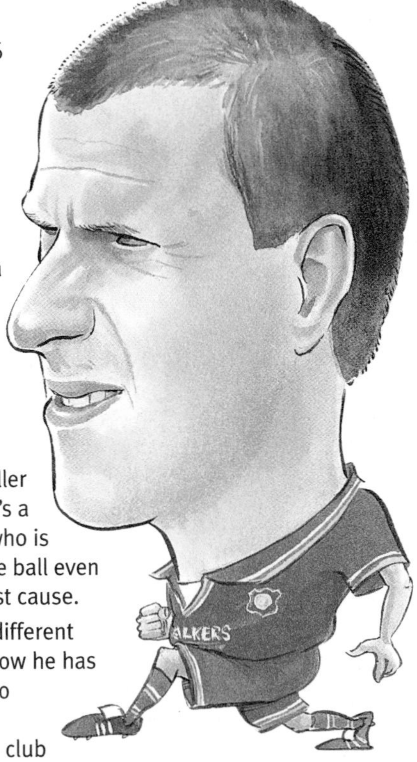

The journeyman-striker has worked his way up division by division and has deservedly made his way into the Premiership. Steve was a major reason why Leicester defied all their critics and comfortably stayed in the Premiership after being promoted.

An untidy looking footballer yet still very effective, he's a very determined player who is never likely to give up the ball even when it seems to be a lost cause.

Leicester is his seventh different club but he hopes that now he has got the respect that he so rightly deserves, he will finish his career with the club that has given him a chance in the top flight.

Matt Elliott

Defender

Place of Birth	Epsom, England
Height	1.86m
Date of Birth	01/11/68
Weight	90kg

One of the bargains of the season and now thought of as one of the Premiership's top defenders.

After having to play in the lower leagues for many years, being watched by lots of clubs who always felt that he could never make it at the top level, Martin O'Neil took a chance and it's a gamble that's paid off handsomely.

His ability in both defending and scoring have given Leicester new ideas and different outlets. He is an inspirational player and others look to him for leadership when their confidence is low.

Leicester City

STATS & FACTS

Club Details

Manager: Martin O'Neill

Assistant Manager: John Robertson

Captain: Steve Walsh

Colours: Home - Blue and White
Away - White and Blue

Ground: Filbert Street

Capacity: 22,517

CLUB HONOURS

League Cup
Winners - 1964, 1997

What are their chances?

After arguably the most successful season in the history of Leicester City, Martin O'Neill has promised that he will build on a team that is bubbling with confidence and full of morale.

With a good blend of youth – Emile Heskey, Muzzie Izzett – and experience – Steve Claridge and Steve Walsh – there is a good basis of a team and with some fresh faces there is no reason why they cannot again achieve mid-table security and enjoy another good cup run.

PAST RECORD

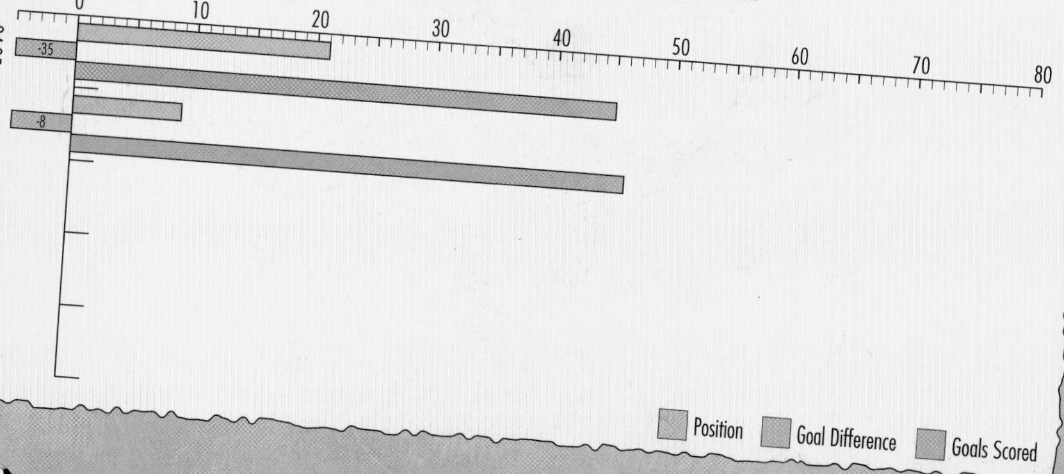

TITLE ODDS

100/1

ON AUGUST 9TH START OF SEASON

Leicester City

TEAM POSITIONS AND LINE-UP

1 KEVIN POOLE	2 SIMON GRAYSON	3 MIKE WHITLOW	4 JULIAN WATTS	5 STEVE WALSH	6 MUZZY IZZET
7 NEIL LENNON	8 SCOTT TAYLOR	9 STEVE CLARIDGE	10 GARRY PARKER	11 EMILE HESKEY	12 MARK ROBINS
13 KASEY KELLER	14 COLIN HILL	15 PONTUS KAAMARK	16 FRANK ROLLING	17 SPENCER PRIOR	18 MATT ELLIOTT
19 ROBERT ULLATHORNE	20 IAN MARSHALL	21 JAMIE LAWRENCE	22 NEIL LEWIS	23 SAM MCMAHON	24 STEVE GUPPY
25 STUART WILSON	26 STUART CAMPBELL	27 STEPHEN WENLOCK	28	29	30 PAUL HYDE
31	32 KEVIN SKELDON	33 MARTIN FOX	34 STEFAN OAKES	35	36

Robbie Fowler

Striker

Place of Birth	Liverpool, England
Height	1.78m
Date of Birth	09/04/75
Weight	75kg

Even though being compared to such prolific goalscorers as Rush, Dalglish and Keegan is flattering, it seems now that at only 22, Robbie Fowler has established himself as a unique talent.

With season 96/97 seeing Robbie score less freely as in past seasons different aspects of his game have been noticed; bringing players into play, running off the ball and setting up many more chances.

With his third full Premiership season behind him he is quickly becoming one of the most complete strikers in the game. It can only be a matter of time before he is called upon to show what he can do on the international scene on a regular basis. Scoring his first international goal against Mexico was a good start.

Player to Watch

Michael Owen

Striker

Place of Birth	Liverpool, England
Height	1.74m
Date of Birth	28/07/79
Weight	70kg

Already talked about by many as being the next Robbie Fowler, Michael is still only a boy of 18. He has made a few substitute appearances, finally making his first full appearance on the last day of the season. He scored his first goal in the previous game after coming on as substitute.

With the form of Fowler and Berger there is plenty of competition for forward places but the manager, Roy Evans, has hinted that Michael's time may soon come.

Again top scorer for the youth team, even if he eventually becomes a first team regular, he will always be remembered for breaking goalscoring records in the Liverpool youth team.

Jamie Redknapp

Midfielder

Place of Birth	Barton On Sea, England
Height	1.80m
Date of Birth	25/6/73
Weight	77kg

The pin-up boy of the Premiership had an awkward season in the 96/97 campaign yet showed that he is still one of the best midfielders in the top flight after some cracking performances during the latter part of the season. Unfortunately, an injury he suffered when playing for England against South Africa may delay his start to the season.

Despite this setback he has established himself in the England squad and it's looking as though he'll get the nod from Glenn Hoddle should England get to the World Cup in France.

The cultured midfielder is under constant transfer speculation and is forever being linked with a move abroad or to London, but he has firmly stated that his future lies with Liverpool and, when fit, he'll be raring to go next season.

David James

Goalkeeper

Place of Birth	Welwyn, England
Height	1.90m
Date of Birth	01/08/70
Weight	90kg

Another flourishing season for the former Watford keeper in which he finally caught the eye of Glenn Hoddle and made that jump into the England team. Many have praised the sturdiness of the Liverpool defence but they seem less inclined to praise the way in which James has contributed to the tightness of the Anfield rearguard.

At the age of 27, he is now a much more mature and competent goalkeeper than the player who was looked upon as a bit of a clown in seasons past; although towards the end of the season he did make some costly mistakes.

Still in his prime David can look towards the future for further national honours but in his first season in a championship race he looks to have relished the pressure producing some quality performances.

Player of the Season

Steve McManaman

Midfielder

Place of Birth	Liverpool, England
Height	1.80m
Date of Birth	11/02/72
Weight	72kg

Liverpool through and through, Steve plays with passion and desire and is adored by the Kop. He is a unique player, incomparable to any other and will live on to be a legend in the Liverpool hall of fame. His ability to cover the whole pitch for 90 minutes is unmatched in the Premiership.

Now a regular in the England squad, he has created his own position by playing in and around the strikers. Even though he is criticised for his lack of goals, his dazzling wing play bamboozles defences and creates openings for Robbie Fowler and others.

Greats of the past have said that players reach their peak at the age of 25 or 26 and Steve, at the age of 25, is now one of the most sought after talents in Europe.

Liverpool

Patrik Berger

Striker

Place of Birth	Prague, Czech Republic
Height	1.87m
Date of Birth	10/11/73
Weight	80kg

A £3.5 million buy during the summer of 96, the Czech pin-up star has set Anfield alight over the past year with some quite devastating performances. Roy Evans has still to make up his mind on where he thinks he can put Patrik to best use but it is obvious that the Euro 96 star is very happy in Liverpool.

Having relegated Patrik to the bench on a few occasions, Roy Evans has commented: 'It is all part of a learning process. Patrik is a quality player but is still learning the English game.'

With his trademark hair band and male model looks he has become quite a hit with the female faithful but, if he can go on producing some stylish performances, the rest of the Anfield crowd will be chanting his name for years to come.

Liverpool

STATS & FACTS

Club Details

Manager: Roy Evans

Assistant Manager: Dougie Livermore

Captain: Mark Wright

Colours: Home - Red
Away - Ecru and Black

Ground: Anfield

Capacity: 45,000

CLUB HONOURS

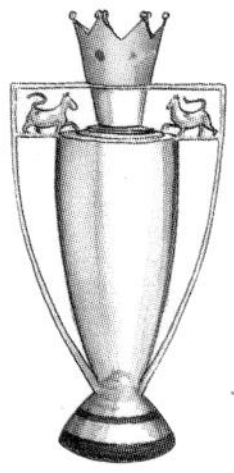

League
Champions - 1900-01, 1905-06, 1921-22, 1922-23, 1946-47, 1963-64, 1965-66, 1972-73, 1975-76, 1976-77, 1978-79, 1979-80, 1981-82, 1982-83, 1983-84, 1985-86, 1987-88, 1989-90

FA Cup
Winners - 1965, 1974, 1986, 1989, 1992

League Cup
Winners - 1981, 1982, 1983, 1984, 1995

European Cup
Winners - 1977, 1978, 1981, 1984

European Super Cup
Winners - 1977

UEFA Cup
Winners - 1973, 1976

What are their chances?

After a year in which they were involved in another fantastic finish to the Premiership season it looks as though Roy Evans and his side will again be challenging for the title. Chances are that Mr. Evans will make a few shrewd signings during the close season especially now that Collymore's controversial Anfield career has come to an end.

With a squad of such depth and quality they are right up there with the best and if they don't achieve championship glory, success in European competition is certainly within reach – Liverpool are beginning to establish themselves as one of the greats in Europe again.

PAST RECORD

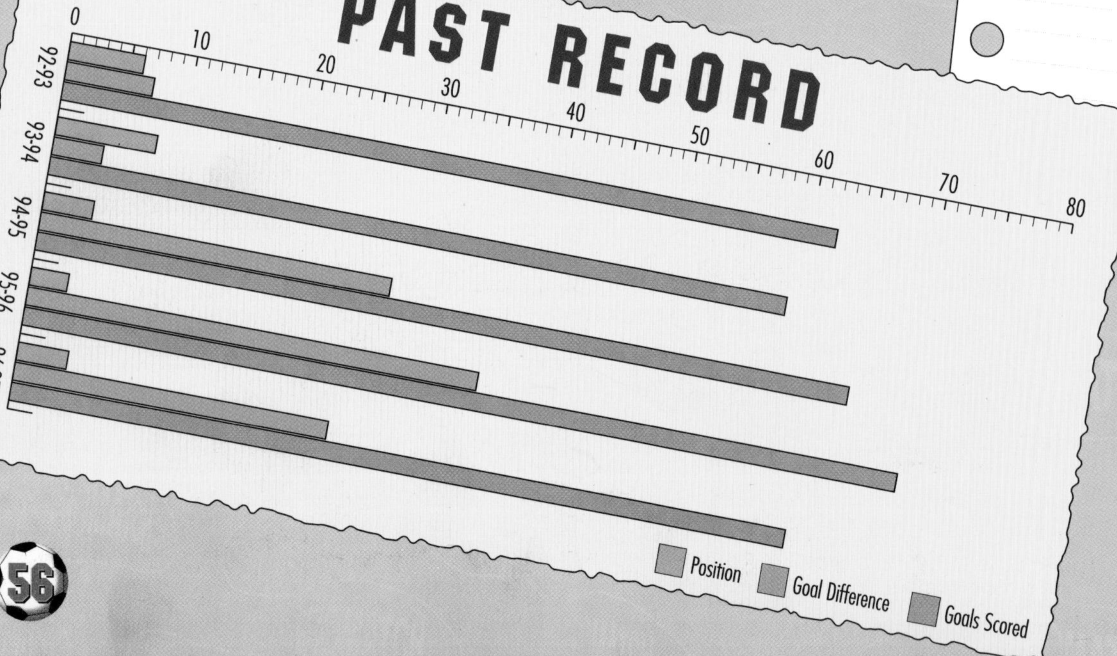

TITLE ODDS

3/1

ON AUGUST 9TH START OF SEASON

Liverpool

TEAM POSITIONS AND LINE-UP

1	DAVID JAMES
2	ROB JONES
3	BJORN TORE KVARME
4	JASON MCATEER
5	MARK WRIGHT
6	PHIL BABB
7	STEVE MCMANAMAN
8	MICHAEL OWEN
9	ROBBIE FOWLER
10	JOHN BARNES
11	JAMIE REDKNAPP
12	STEVE HARKNESS
13	TONY WARNER
14	NEIL RUDDOCK
15	PATRIK BERGER
16	MICHAEL THOMAS
17	MICHAEL OWEN
18	
19	MARK KENNEDY
20	STIG INGE BJORNEBYE
21	DOMINIC MATTEO
22	JAMIE CASSIDY
23	JAMIE CARRAGHER
24	LEE JONES
25	DAVID THOMPSON
26	
27	
28	
29	
30	
31	
32	
33	
34	
35	
36	

Roy Keane

Midfielder

Place of Birth	Cork, Eire
Height	1.78m
Date of Birth	10/08/71
Weight	81kg

When the United faithful saw Paul Ince leave for Milan in 1995 many were worried where the fight and spirit in the midfield would come from. Little did they know the emergence of the fiery Irishman would be so great.

His ability to cover so much of the pitch in a match is quite amazing and with his effort and commitment, along with an abundance of skill and vision, he's the linchpin in the United side.

Roy does have that grit about him which sometimes leads him into trouble but he would not feel he could give the same commitment if that fight was not shown in his play. The only problem his manager may have is that, at the prime age of 26, Roy may be tempted by the idea of playing on the continent where players of his style are so desperately needed.

Andy Cole

Striker

Place of Birth	Nottingham, England
Height	1.78m
Date of Birth	15/10/71
Weight	72kg

After his record breaking £7 million move in 1995, Andy seems to have finally settled in at Old Trafford and with Monsieur Cantona retiring, it looks as though the England international is going to be given a regular starting place.

After scoring those 40 goals in a season on Tyneside, Andy has never really hit that form for United yet he has had a run of painful injuries which have limited his appearances.

With intense competition for places in the United forward line Andy is glad to know that he now has England recognition and that is something that Alex Ferguson will note when selecting his team for the first day of the season.

Player to Watch

Paul Scholes

Striker

Place of Birth	Salford, England
Height	1.72m
Date of Birth	16/11/74
Weight	67kg

Even though the nippy forward has been beginning to break into the team over the last few seasons, we feel that it will be in the future when Paul shows he is the one to take over the prized reigns of Eric Cantona. He may not have the same flamboyance as the Frenchman but he makes up for that in pace and determination.

The 96/97 season forced him to watch quite a lot from the sidelines, either from niggling injuries or because of the form of Solskjaer. Yet his performances when he played were highly impressive and Paul often featured in a midfield role, showing that Mr. Ferguson had enough confidence in Paul to play him in such a demanding role.

Ole Gunnar Solskjaer

Striker

Place of Birth Kristiansund, Norway
Height 1.78m
Date of Birth 26/02/73
Weight 74kg

The 'baby faced assassin' is how this youthful striker is often described. His deadly finishing meant he had a remarkable first Premiership season. He arrived at Old Trafford last summer from Norweigan club Molde for a fee of £1.5 million, yet not much was expected of him this season.

But his speed, quick reactions, and classy finishing have earned him rave reviews and have also kept £7 million man Andy Cole waiting on the sidelines for his opportunity.

The United Supremo Alex Ferguson said: 'He was not initially bought for this season (96/97) but he has come on leaps and bounds and surprised us all around the club, he is going to be one for the future!'

Player of the Season

David Beckham

Midfielder

Place of Birth Leytonstone, England
Height 1.83m
Date of Birth 02/05/75
Weight 71kg

As a 'Fergie fledgling' David seemed as though he would take time to develop yet his progress last season has astonished many around the country. While Tottenham did not feel David had what it takes, United saw that he had the potential and how the north London club must regret missing out.

David's been put into the same bracket as Bobby Charlton and it seems as though he can only go from strength to strength. From day one of the Premiership 96/97, where he scored that wonder goal at Selhurst Park, he seems to have grown in stature, maturity and skill.

He has now taken on a cosmopolitan status enjoyed by so many young football stars. But while many young players have let off-the-field distractions affect their form, David has shown increasing maturity repaying the trust Alex Ferguson has shown in him. Now he's established on the international scene, we can only sit back and enjoy the rise and rise of David Beckham.

Manchester United

Ryan Giggs

Striker

Place of Birth Cardiff, Wales
Height 1.80m
Date of Birth 29/11/73
Weight 67kg

When critics seem to punish Ryan Giggs for drifting in and out of games and seemingly lacking passion, many forget that he is only approaching 24. He has been featuring in the United first team squad now for eight years, startling, as people now think of him as one of the senior players.

His goalscoring count in the last season was not what it should be but much of his play went unnoticed - running off the ball, endless assists and superb support play.

Despite constantly being eyed by Italian giants Milan, and having a price tag of over £10 million on his head, he has made it perfectly clear all along that he wants to stay at Old Trafford for the rest of his career.

Manchester United

STATS & FACTS

Club Details

Manager: Alex Ferguson

Assistant Manager: Brian Kidd

Captain: Peter Schmeichel

Colours: Home - Red and White

Away - White and Black

Ground: Old Trafford

Capacity: 55,000

CLUB HONOURS

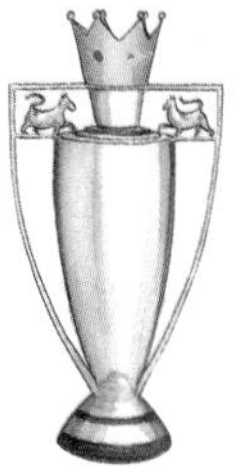

League
Champions - 1907-08, 1910-11, 1951-52, 1955-56, 1956-57, 1964-65, 1966-67, 1992-93, 1993-94, 1995-96, 1996-97

FA Cup
Winners - 1909, 1948, 1963, 1977, 1983, 1985, 1990, 1994, 1996

League Cup
Winners - 1992

European Cup
Winners - 1968

European Cup Winners Cup
Winners - 1991

European Super Cup
Winners - 1991

What are their chances?

After years of dominating the Premiership, before finally making their mark in Europe, there is not much that can be said about the future of Manchester United other than it looks as bright and successful as the past half a decade has been.

With the world class players that they now have in their squad, and with the United youth development programme still producing youngsters of the class of Giggs, Beckham and Scholes, a prosperous and rich future looks likely.

Boring as it may seem to many, the truth is that the United team of the 90s goes down with Liverpool in the 80s and the United of the 60s as one of the great forces in English football. Another title looks likely.

PAST RECORD

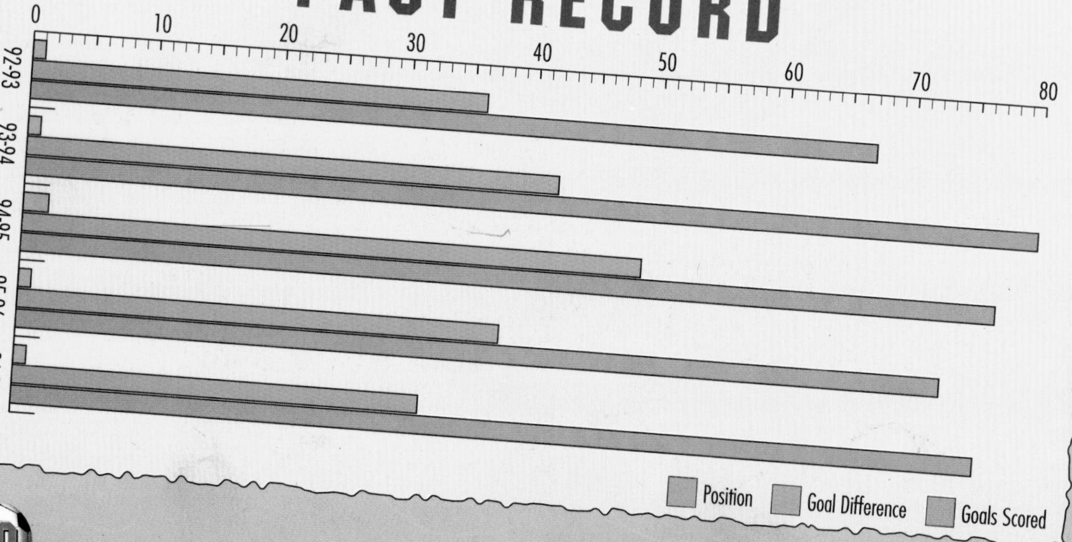

TITLE ODDS

9/4

ON AUGUST 9TH START OF SEASON

Manchester United

TEAM POSITIONS AND LINE-UP

1	2	3	4	5	6
PETER SCHMEICHEL	GARY NEVILLE	DENIS IRWIN	DAVID MAY		GARY PALLISTER
7	8	9	10	11	12
	NICKY BUTT	ANDY COLE	DAVID BECKHAM	RYAN GIGGS	PHIL NEVILLE
13	14	15	16	17	18
BRIAN MCCLAIR	JORDI CRUYFF	KAREL POBORSKY	ROY KEANE	RAYMOND VAN DER GOUW	PAUL SCHOLES
19	20	21	22	23	24
RONNY JOHNSEN	OLE GUNNAR SOLSKJAER		SIMON DAVIES	BEN THORNLEY	JOHN O'KANE
25	26	27	28	29	30
KEVIN PILKINGTON	CHRIS CASPER	TERRY COOKE		MICHAEL APPLETON	
31	32	33	34	35	36
	MICHAEL CLEGG				

David Batty

Midfielder

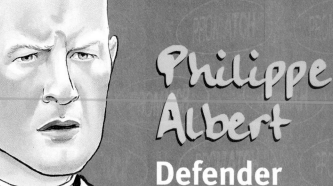

Place of Birth	Leeds, England	Height 1.70m
Date of Birth	02/12/68	Weight 67kg

Whatever is said about some of the more committed parts of David's game he has again proved why he is so highly thought of by top-flight managers. In his first full season in a Newcastle shirt he has become a firm favourite with the crowd, which really comes as no surprise considering his infectious attitude and his incredible desire to win.

Seen as the typical anchor man, he has proved over the last season and a half that he has a lot more to his game. Kevin Keegan once said of him: 'Many people think of him as just a hard man but the amount of skill and vision that he possesses is extraordinary.'

Now his England squad place is secure he can not only help Newcastle in their fight to prove themselves in Europe but will also help his country to a World Cup place.

Philippe Albert

Defender

Place of Birth	Bouillon, Belgium
Height	1.90m
Date of Birth	10/08/67
Weight	90kg

Now in his third season in the Premiership there's less pressure on Philippe to prove himself. He's now much more relaxed in his play.

Still probably the most cultured centre back in the country he possesses a sweet touch and is able to get forward and play in the middle of the park. Yet because of his adventurous style he, along with the rest of his team, is often criticised for conceding silly goals due to a lack of defensive cover.

Captain of the Belgian team on numerous occasions he can hopefully look forward to facing several of his team mates in the World Cup competition of 98.

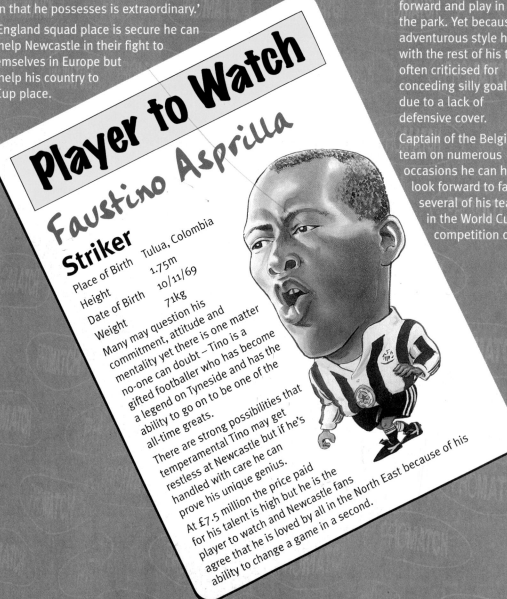

Player to Watch

Faustino Asprilla

Striker

Place of Birth	Tulua, Colombia
Height	1.75m
Date of Birth	10/11/69
Weight	71kg

Many may question his commitment, attitude and mentality yet there is one matter no-one can doubt – Tino is a gifted footballer who has become a legend on Tyneside and has the ability to go on to be one of the all-time greats.

There are strong possibilities that temperamental Tino may get restless at Newcastle but if he's handled with care he can prove his unique genius.

At £7.5 million the price paid for his talent is high but he is the player to watch and Newcastle fans agree that he is loved by all in the North East because of his ability to change a game in a second.

Robert Lee

Midfielder

Place of Birth London, England
Height 1.78m
Date of Birth 01/02/66
Weight 76kg

1996/97 saw Robert have one of his best campaigns so far and, having notched over 10 goals, he is probably one of the most consistent attacking midfielders in the Premiership. By forcing himself back into the England squad after some disappointing performances he is now looking forward to possibly going to France in 1998.

With Ferdinand, Shearer and Asprilla injured on occasions there were times when Robert found himself playing up front where he gave very creditable performances.

Costing £750,000 three years ago, he is probably one of the all-time bargain buys and other managers around the country are praying they can find someone of his quality for the same value.

Player of the Season

Alan Shearer

Striker

Place of Birth
Newcastle-upon-Tyne, England
Height 1.80m
Date of Birth 13/08/70
Weight 79kg

Few English players in the past 20 years have reached Alan Shearer's level of achievement. Now regarded by many as one of the best strikers in the world, along with Ronaldo and George Weah, he can look back on a career that has brought him so much success by the age of 27.

His record breaking £15 million move in the summer of 96 from Blackburn to Tyneside made many feel that the pressure of being the world's most expensive player would adversely affect Alan's form. Maybe the goals would be harder to come by. But with his goals to games ratio being one every 1.5 games, he has defied such critics.

Despite his swaggering destruction of opposition defences, he's a very level-headed man off the pitch. The trappings of succcess haven't spoiled Alan.

Les Ferdinand

Striker

Place of Birth London, England
Height 1.80m
Date of Birth 18/12/66
Weight 85kg

The arrival of Alan Shearer took a lot of the pressure off Les, who himself cost £6 million the previous season. Certainly his partnership with Shearer met all expectations.

Goals have been expected by the demanding Newcastle fans, yet Les no longer has to carry the goalscoring burden now he has an even more prolific striking partner.

There is no doubt that he still is one of the top strikers in the game and by scoring once again over 20 goals, he remains the type of player most managers would pick to lead their attack. Whether Kenny Dalglish will retain his services is another matter.

Newcastle United

STATS & FACTS

Club Details

Manager: Kenny Dalglish

Assistant Manager: Terry McDermott

Captain: Robert Lee

Colours: Home - Black and White

Away - Light Blue and Black

Ground: St James' Park

Capacity: 36,610

CLUB HONOURS

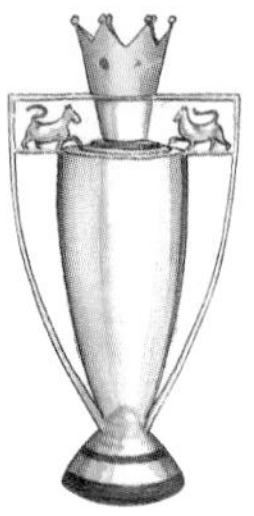

League
Champions - 1904-05, 1906-07, 1908-09, 1926-27

FA Cup
Winners - 1910, 1924, 1932, 1951, 1952, 1955

UEFA Cup
Winners - 1969

What are their chances?

Every year there is a new and optimistic reason why Newcastle can win the title; the arrival of Les Ferdinand one year and then Alan Shearer and now it's Kenny Dalglish, who is starting his first full season in charge.

Taking over during the middle of the 96/97 season it was felt that it was too soon to expect immediate results from him but now, with a fresh season, he can make Newcastle his own team rather than a legacy of Kevin Keegan's.

There is no doubt that they will challenge once again and will look to the cups for glory.

PAST RECORD

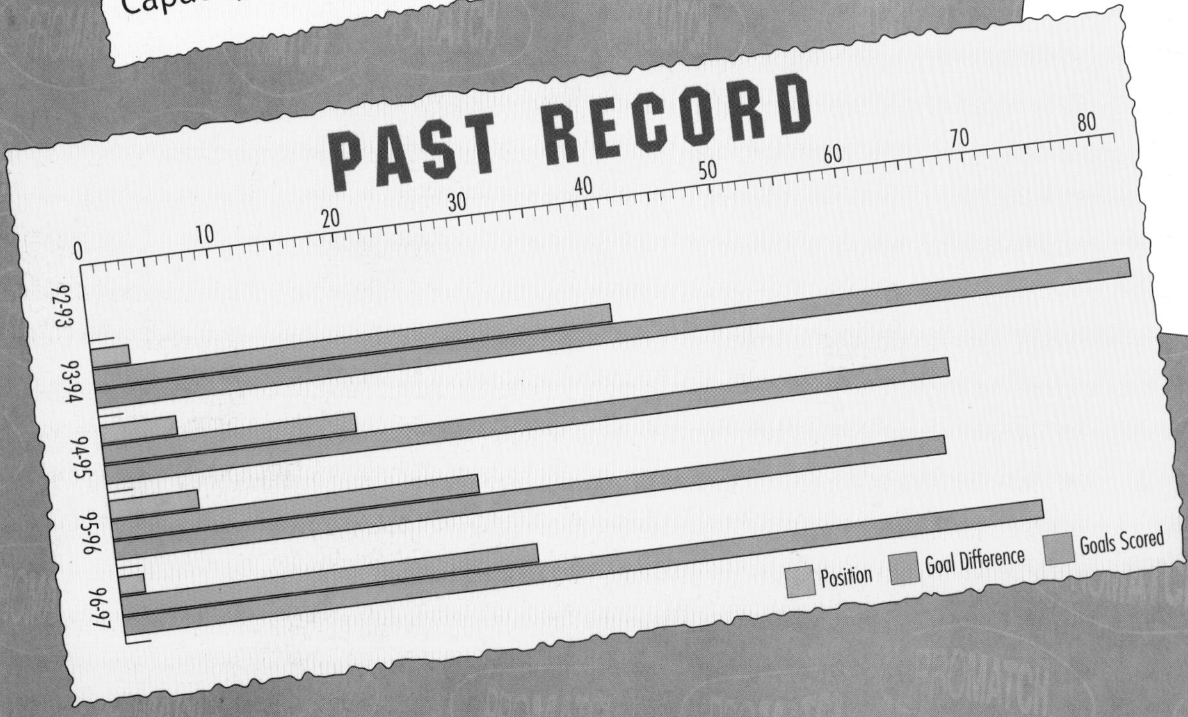

TITLE ODDS

6/1

ON AUGUST 9TH START OF SEASON

Newcastle United

TEAM POSITIONS AND LINE-UP

1 PAVEL SRNICEK	2 WARREN BARTON	3 JOHN BERESFORD	4 DAVID BATTY	5 DARREN PEACOCK	6 STEVE HOWEY
7 ROBERT LEE	8 PETER BEARDSLEY	9 ALAN SHEARER	10 LES FERDINAND	11 FAUSTINO ASPRILLA	12 DES HAMILTON
13	14 DAVID GINOLA	15 SHAKA HISLOP	16	17 JIMMY CRAWFORD	18 KEITH GILLESPIE
19 STEVE WATSON	20	21	22	23	24
25 PAUL BRAYSON	26 ROBBIE ELLIOT	27 PHILIPPE ALBERT	28	29	30
31	32	33	34	35	36

Des Walker

Defender

Place of Birth	Hackney, England
Height	1.78m
Date of Birth	26/11/65
Weight	72kg

After being regarded as the best defender in Europe before being totally discarded and written off, he has shown once again that he still has what it takes to play in one of the best leagues in the world.

His speed and marking have always been his main attributes and yet, with the years creeping up on him, it still seems as though he has retained the pace that he showed in his Forest days.

After losing so much confidence one of the quiet men in football had one of his best seasons in the 96/97 campaign and there has been talk of a possible international recall.

Regi Blinker

Midfielder

Place of Birth	Surinam
Height	1.73m
Date of Birth	04/06/69
Weight	73kg

One of the bargains of the Premiership at only £250,000 from Feyenoord, he now seems quite priceless to the Hillsborough side.

When brought in he transformed the side and added the touch of class that his team was so desperately lacking. Even though his skills and pace are quite breathtaking he has found it difficult to play a full English season, enduring a demanding schedule that he has not been used to.

Many fans hope that they see the dreadlocked Dutchman in a Wednesday shirt next year yet there is talk that he may move away. It would be another team's gain but Sheffield Wednesday's loss.

Player to Watch

Andy Booth

Striker

Place of Birth	Huddersfield, England
Height	1.86m
Date of Birth	17/03/73
Weight	79kg

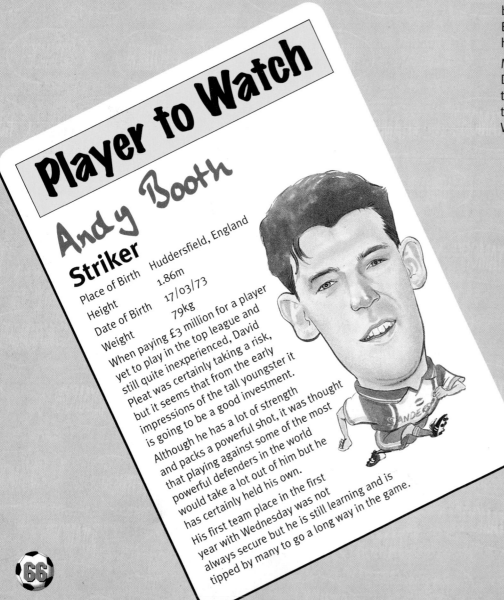

When paying £3 million for a player yet to play in the top league and still quite inexperienced, David Pleat was certainly taking a risk, but it seems that from the early impressions of the tall youngster it is going to be a good investment.

Although he has a lot of strength and packs a powerful shot, it was thought that playing against some of the most powerful defenders in the world would take a lot out of him but he has certainly held his own.

His first team place in the first year with Wednesday was not always secure but he is still learning and is tipped by many to go a long way in the game.

Sheffield Wednesday

Mark Pembridge

Midfielder

Place of Birth	Merthyr Tydfil, Wales
Height	1.70m
Date of Birth	29/11/70
Weight	71kg

The sturdy Welshman has now achieved what he always wanted, to become a regular in a Premiership side after having to play in the First Division for many years. Along the way he's also suffered some terrible injuries.

Regarded as one of the complete midfielders in the league with good vision and distribution and with a terrier-like attitude.

He became a very important player on the side in the 96/97 campaign, where he was relied upon to win the ball back as well as add a few goals himself. He performed both roles very well.

Player of the Season

Kevin Pressman

Goalkeeper

Place of Birth	Fareham, England
Height	1.86m
Date of Birth	06/11/67
Weight	90kg

At the beginning of the 96/97 campaign David Pleat was heavily criticised for producing a team that offered little in the way of flair. What he did produce was a team that proved that hard work and commitment can achieve success. There is no-one who demonstrates the traits of determination and commitment more than Kevin Pressman.

After having to handle stick from the Wednesday crowd in seasons past, he had his best-ever year, helping the Owls achieve a top seven finish. Kevin was one of the main reasons why his team was so difficult to beat.

His manager has stressed how disappointed he was that Kevin has yet to be given international recognition because he is a goalkeeper who really does thrive in the pressurised atmosphere of the Premiership.

Benito Carbone

Midfielder

Place of Birth	Bagnara, Italy
Height	1.73m
Date of Birth	14/08/71
Weight	72kg

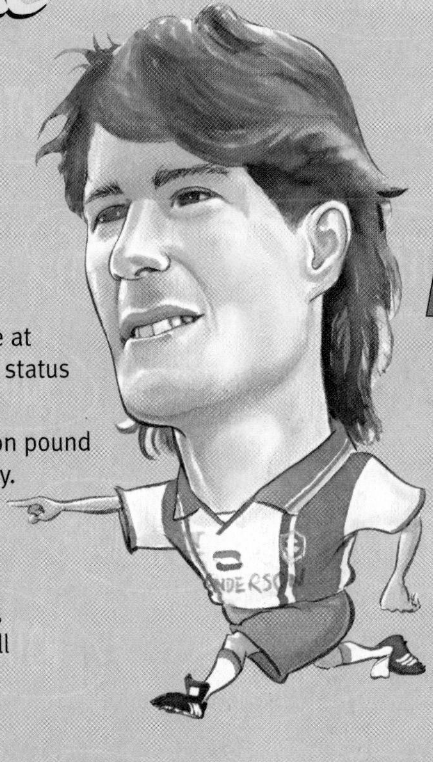

The arrival of Italian stars such as Ravanelli and Zola completely overshadowed the arrival of Benito Carbone at Hillsborough. His countrymen had a more star-studded status yet Benito has shown that he has just as much quality.

David Pleat brought Benito to Sheffield in a multi-million pound deal and so far he seems to have paid back every penny.

His first touch and marvellous ability is only to be admired and learned from. He seems to have settled in really well, looking as though he enjoys his football. The Wednesday fans have certainly enjoyed his quality, recognising that Benito has provided much-needed skill in the middle of the park.

Sheffield Wednesday

STATS & FACTS

Club Details

Manager: David Pleat

Assistant Manager: Peter Shreeves

Captain: Peter Atherton

Colours: Home - Blue and White

Away - Green and White

Ground: Hillsborough

Capacity: 39,814

CLUB HONOURS

League
Champions - 1902-03, 1903-04, 1928-29, 1929-30

FA Cup
Winners - 1896, 1907, 1935

League Cup
Winners - 1991

What are their chances?

After being tipped to struggle in past seasons there are few who are now ready to write off David Pleat's side for the coming season.

He has now got a team that work hard for each other and also has a good balance between muscular players and those with the skill.

A push for the championship is still not within their reach but the relegation worries are unlikely to surface and Wednesday are definitely a good bet for a cup this year.

PAST RECORD

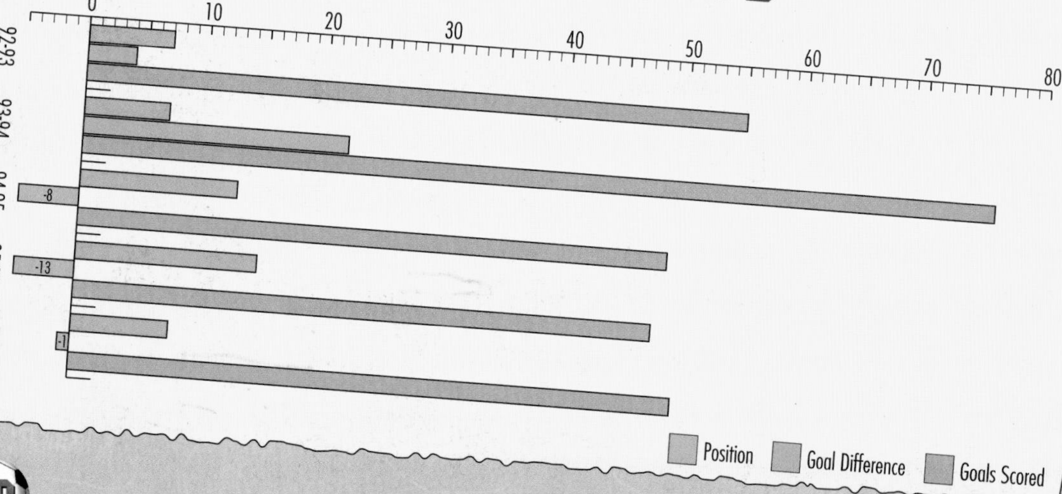

TITLE ODDS

40/1

ON AUGUST 9TH START OF SEASON

Sheffield Wednesday

TEAM POSITIONS AND LINE-UP

1 KEVIN PRESSMAN	2 PETER ATHERTON	3 IAN NOLAN	4 MARK PEMBRIDGE	5 JON NEWSOME	6 DES WALKER
7 GUY WHITTINGHAM	8	9 DAVID HIRST	10 ANDY BOOTH	11 REGI BLINKER	12 GRAHAM HYDE
13 MATT CLARKE	14 STEVE NICOL	15	16	17 LEE BRISCOE	18 DEJAN STEFANOVIC
19 SCOTT OAKES	20 WAYNE COLLINS	21	22 O'NEILL DONALDSON	23	24
25 RICHIE HUMPHREYS	26 ORLANDO TRUSTFULL	27	28 BENITO CARBONE	29	30
31	32	33	34	35	36

Matthew Le Tissier

Striker

Place of Birth Guernsey, Channel Islands
Height 1.86m
Date of Birth 14/10/68
Weight 81kg

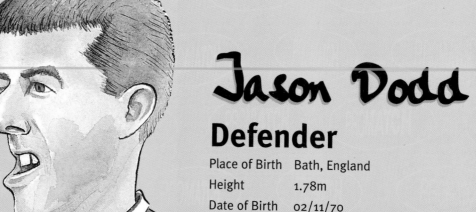

Even though he did not have one of his most consistent seasons there was still no doubting his ability and he showed on many an occasion why he is thought of as having one of the most cultured right feet in the English game.

The goals didn't come as thick and fast as he would have liked yet the plus side for him in the 96/97 season was that he managed to eventually force his way back into the England squad, appearing in the crucial World Cup game against Italy.

After spending his entire career at the Saints it now seems unlikely that he will ever move elsewhere. He is sure to go down in the history books as one of the most influential and talented players Southampton has ever had.

Jason Dodd

Defender

Place of Birth Bath, England
Height 1.78m
Date of Birth 02/11/70
Weight 76kg

Although not one of the Premiership's star players, he is thought of as one of the most underrated full-backs in the Premiership and it looks as though he may be on his way out of the Dell in a big money move to a top club.

Having worked his way up through the ranks at Southampton he has made the right-back slot his own yet on occasion he has been asked to move to the centre of defence where he is just as useful.

He has speed, great technique and a powerful shot that has seen him reach double figures in goals during his time in the top flight.

Player to Watch

Eyal Berkovic

Midfielder

Place of Birth Haifa, Israel
Height 1.75m
Date of Birth 02/04/72
Weight 76kg

Having taken the Dell by storm with some absolutely outstanding performances in his first season in the English game, he is being tipped by many to become one of the most accomplished midfielders in Europe - good news for him yet bad news for Southampton who are resigned to the fact that top clubs in Europe are hot on Eyal's heels.

The diminutive Israeli has wonderful vision and distribution and, along with a vicious shot, he really is one of the best imports in the Premiership.

As well as playing a major part in helping Southampton stay in the top flight he has also shown that he has got what it takes to play on the international scene with Israel, who seem likely to qualify for the World Cup in 98.

Southampton

Jim Magilton

Midfielder

Place of Birth Belfast, Northern Ireland

Height 1.78m

Date of Birth 06/05/69

Weight 79kg

Southampton's playmaker in the middle of the park was just as determined and inspirational as he has ever been and played a major part in helping Southampton survive yet one more year in the top flight.

When out of the side, either with injury or when dropped, it always seemed that there was something missing from the Saints' midfield. When Jim was in the side it was as though they had more ideas and chances to score.

The former Oxford man has made his name as one of the most accomplished midfielders in the Premiership and it's likely he will be asked to play a more holding role in the middle of the park.

Player of the Season

Egil Ostenstadt

Striker

Place of Birth Haugesend, Norway

Height 1.81m

Date of Birth 02/01/72

Weight 79kg

When bought midway through the 96/97 season many Saints fans were unsure about the qualities of the Norwegian striker yet he has proved to be one of the buys of the season and is now being looked at by clubs all over Europe.

Graeme Souness brought him for a bargain £800,000 and the deal immediately paid dividends with Egil scoring over ten goals including a hat-trick against Manchester United in their 6-3 drubbing.

He has a great first touch and has a real eye for a goal and even though up to now he's been an unknown in the world of football, the Norwegian international is now seen as one of the most dangerous strikers in the Premiership.

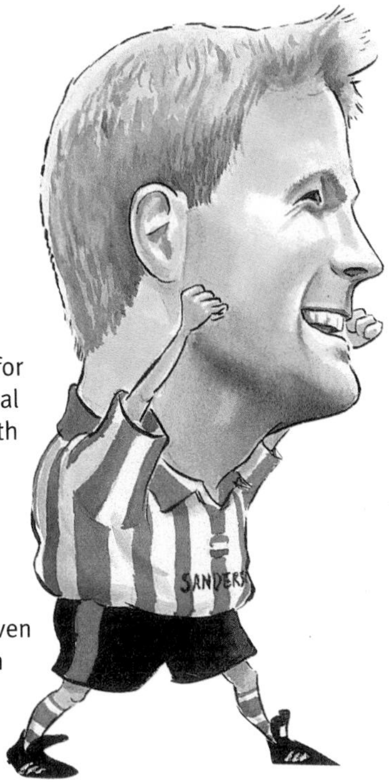

Maik Taylor

Goalkeeper

Place of Birth Germany

Height 1.94m

Date of Birth 04/09/71

Weight 91kg

It always seemed as though Southampton had struggled in the past with the goalkeeper's slot, yet Graeme Souness was determined to put that right and it seems that his ability to pluck players from the lower leagues has come up trumps again with the signing of the talented Maik Taylor.

Bought from Barnet after a third of the season he has performed heroics; after only having had experience in the Third Division it is quite astonishing to see how comfortably he has settled into the fast tempo of the Premiership.

At only 26 he is reasonably young for a keeper and if he maintains his form then interest from German supremo Berti Vogts is not out of the question in the future.

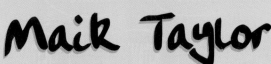

Southampton

STATS & FACTS

Club Details

Manager: Dave Jones

Assistant Managers: John Mortimore, Terry Cooper

Captain: Matt Le Tissier

Colours: Home - Red, White and Black

Away - Blue and Yellow

Ground: The Dell

Capacity: 15,000

CLUB HONOURS

FA Cup
Winners - 1976

What are their chances?

The shock of Graeme Souness' resignation shook the Dell to its foundations. Saints' fans were outraged, believing that with Souness at the helm they had a chance of success.

With or without Souness, the defence needs to be improved and a top quality striker should be found to play alongside Ostenstadt.

If these changes aren't made, then it looks as though their luck could run out and Southampton may face the dreaded drop.

PAST RECORD

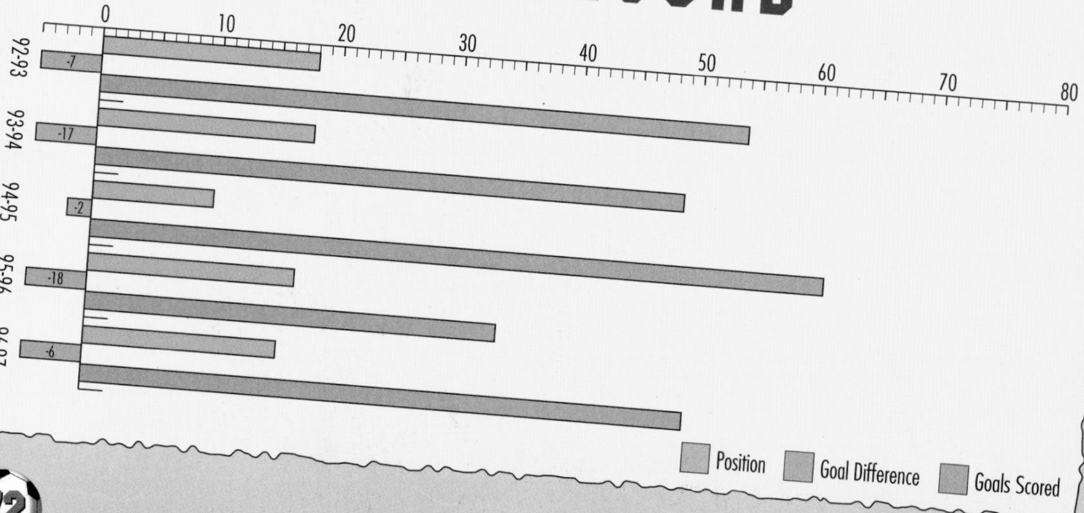

TITLE ODDS
200/1
ON AUGUST 9TH START OF SEASON

Southampton

TEAM POSITIONS AND LINE-UP

1 DAVE BEASANT
2 JASON DODD
3 FRANCIS BENALI
4 JIM MAGILTON
5 BARRY VENISON
6 KEN MONKOU
7 MATT LE TISSIER
8
9
10 NEIL MADDISON
11
12 GRAHAM POTTER
13 NEIL MOSS
14 SIMON CHARLTON
15 ALAIN NEILSON
16 DAVID HUGHES
17 PAUL TISDALE
18 MATT OAKLEY
19 RICHARD DRYDEN
20 ROBBIE SLATER
21
22 KLAUS LUNDEKVAM
23
24 CHRIS WARREN
25 PAUL SHEERIN
26 MATT ROBINSON
27 STEVE BASHAM
28
29 EYAL BERKOVIC
30 EGIL OSTENSTADT
31
32 ULRICH VAN GOBBEL
33 MAIK TAYLOR
34
35
36

Darren Anderton

Midfielder

Place of Birth	Southampton, England
Height	1.86m
Date of Birth	03/03/72
Weight	75kg

After suffering yet another season of horrendous injuries, when he did play, he showed that he is still one of the most talented players in the country.

Darren's injuries have been a major factor in Gerry Francis' failure to bring back the glory days to Tottenham. Darren is such an instrumental player in the middle of the park, and his ability to pick a player out with a pass is quite outstanding.

'Shaggy', as he is nicknamed, is now reaching the stage of his career (he's 25) when he should be at his peak. And if he can get back to full fitness, then the best of Darren is yet to come.

Player to Watch

Rory Allen

Striker

Place of Birth	Beckenham, England
Height	1.83m
Date of Birth	17/10/77
Weight	71kg

During the 96/97 season Spurs had their main strikers, Sheringham, Armstrong and Iverson all missing through injury and had to rely on youngsters such as Rory Allen. Inexperienced, and not yet physically able to cope with life in the Premiership, he still showed that he has the ability to go a long way in the game.

When he's stronger and fitter – maybe after a loan spell at a lower division club for experience – he certainly has the talent to do what another Allen, Clive, (no relation!) did in his Tottenham days.

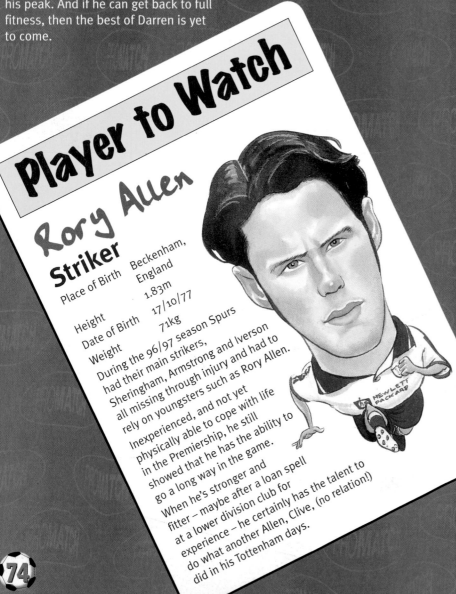

Teddy Sheringham

Striker

Place of Birth	Highams Park, England
Height	1.83m
Date of Birth	02/04/66
Weight	78kg

Yet another player who had an injury-plagued season but he's still shown he has the class to be one of the top strikers in the Premiership.

At 31, Teddy still seems to be on the top of his game by playing in his own role. He floats around the pitch, linking defence and attack, and appears in some unusual positions, sometimes he is even the last man!

There has been talk of Teddy moving on from White Hart Lane, yet as captain, it seems as though he feels that he has the inspiration and skill to guide Spurs to success in the coming season.

Tottenham Hotspur

Stefan Iverson

Striker

Place of Birth	Oslo, Norway
Height	1.80m
Date of Birth	10/11/76
Weight	77kg

After impressing many managers around Europe with some fantastic performances in the Champions League for Norwegian club Rosenborg, it was Gerry Francis who came in with £2.5 million to capture the 19 year-old.

Since his arrival he's scored over 10 goals and really has become a favourite with the fans, his pace and eye for goal have seen him likened to Marco Van Basten by football pundits around the country.

At only 19, he has a really exciting future, and with players such as Sheringham and Armstrong around him, he has the assistance of experienced Premiership strikers to help him become one of the top marksmen in Europe.

Player of the Season

Sol Campbell

Defender

Place of Birth	Newham, England
Height	1.83m
Date of Birth	18/09/74
Weight	76kg

Having now played well over one hundred games for the Spurs, Sol is one of the first names on Gerry Francis' teamsheet and deservedly so.

Also a regular fixture in the England squad, Sol was by far the most outstanding player for Spurs in the 96/97 campaign and seemed to control a defence decimated by terrible injuries.

He has pace, strength and a great reading of the game which are the reasons why he is rated as one of the best defenders in the country. There is no doubt that he will get better with experience and will become a permanent fixture in the England team.

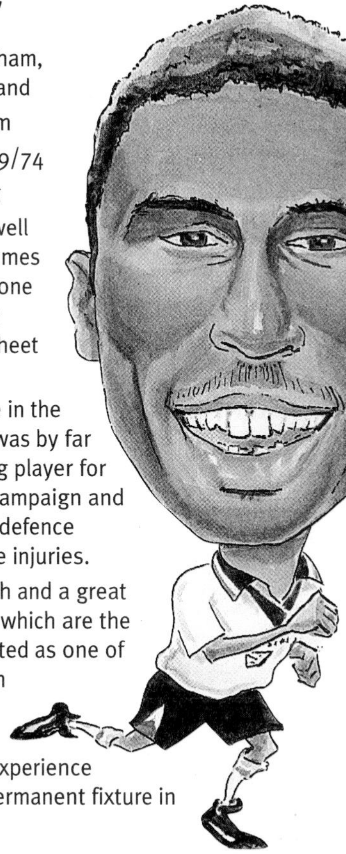

John Scales

Defender

Place of Birth	Harrogate, England
Height	1.88m
Date of Birth	04/07/66
Weight	79kg

When Gerry Francis dived in to sign John Scales from Liverpool halfway through the 96/97 season, it shocked many. It had seemed the ex-Wimbledon defender was to sign for Leeds in a multi-million pound deal.

Even though he struggled with injury during the first month of his career at White Hart Lane, he has been one of Spurs' most consistent players. He looks like the player that Spurs have needed in the centre of defence to play with Sol Campbell.

One of the most articulate players in football, he does seem much happier in London after finding it hard to get a regular place at Liverpool, where there is an abundance of good centre backs.

Tottenham Hotspur

STATS & FACTS

Club Details

Manager: Gerry Francis

Assistant Manager: Roger Cross

Captain: David Howells

Colours: Home - White and Navy Blue

Away - Yellow and Blue

Ground: White Hart Lane

Capacity: 33,083

CLUB HONOURS

League
Champions - 1950-51, 1960-61

FA Cup
Winners - 1901, 1921, 1961, 1962, 1967, 1981, 1982, 1991

League Cup
Winners - 1971, 1973

European Cup Winners Cup
Winners - 1963

UEFA Cup
Winners - 1972, 1984

What are their chances?

Gerry Francis has woken up to the fact that his squad needed strengthening; with new players such as Iverson, Scales and Vega, Spurs now have players with plenty of ability and there are sure to be more to follow with Alan Sugar's millions hopefully available to spend.

In seasons past, Spurs fans have always felt optimistic at the beginning of the season and with fresh faces and players returning from long-term injuries, Gerry will at last be able to get his first choice line-up on the pitch.

Spurs for one of the cups.

PAST RECORD

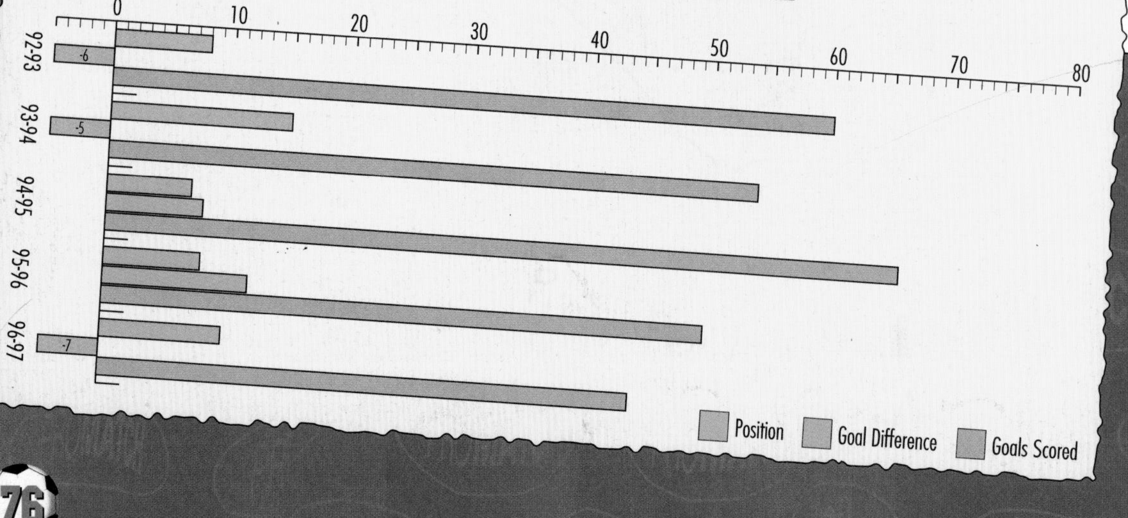

TITLE ODDS
80/1
ON AUGUST 9TH START OF SEASON

Tottenham Hotspur

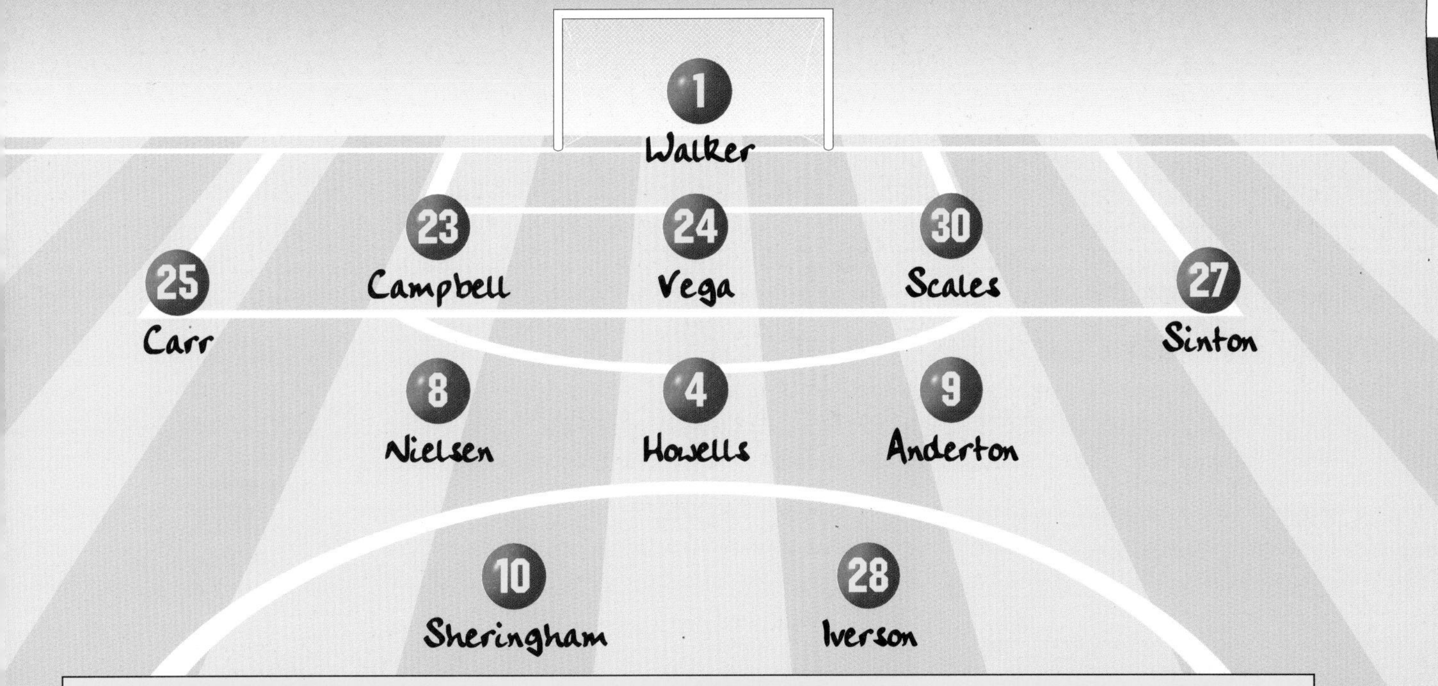

TEAM POSITIONS AND LINE-UP

1	2	3	4	5	6
IAN WALKER	DEAN AUSTIN	JUSTIN EDINBURGH	DAVID HOWELLS	COLIN CALDERWOOD	GARY MABBUTT
7	8	9	10	11	12
RUEL FOX	ALAN NIELSEN	DARREN ANDERTON	TEDDY SHERINGHAM	CHRIS ARMSTRONG	JASON DOZZELL
13	14	15	16	17	18
ESPEN BAARDSEN	STUART NETHERCOTT	CLIVE WILSON		NEALE FENN	
19	20	21	22	23	24
		DANNY HILL		SOL CAMPBELL	RAMON VEGA
25	26	27	28	29	30
STEVE CARR	PAUL MAHORN	ANDY SINTON	STEPHAN IVERSON	RORY ALLEN	JOHN SCALES
31	32	33	34	35	36
SIMON BROWN					

Steve Lomas

Midfielder

Place of Birth	Hannover, Germany
Height	1.80m
Date of Birth	18/01/74
Weight	80kg

Brought in on the transfer deadline day during the 1996/7 campaign he's proved that he already has what it takes to play in the Premiership.

After coming through the ranks at Manchester City he became a favourite with the crowd, his tenacity and rough-and-ready attitude showed the Maine Road faithful his true commitment to the cause of the team.

Harry Redknapp came in for the Northern Ireland international, needing a ballwinner in his team, and saw that Steve was going to be the perfect player to slot into that role.

John Hartson

Striker

Place of Birth	Swansea, Wales
Height	1.80m
Date of Birth	05/04/75
Weight	75kg

When Harry Redknapp saw that he had made a mistake in bringing foreigners such as Raducioiu and Futre to Upton Park he found himself with a lack of strikers. Arsenal's John Hartson was first on Harry's list when he decided who he wanted to lead the Hammer's front line.

The fiery Welsh striker could eventually cost the Hammers £5million; many thought the price was too high to pay for someone of John's calibre, yet he showed the fans and the critics that he has the ability. He is now well on the way to becoming one of the top strikers in the country.

He is tall, strong and quick and is a constant menace for opposing teams. Only 22 years-old, he has a bright future and he is hoping that he can help score the goals that could make West Ham a side to be reckoned with.

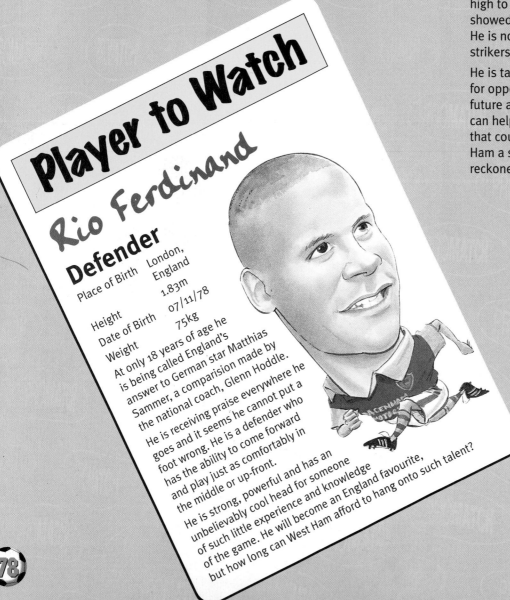

Player to Watch

Rio Ferdinand

Defender

Place of Birth	London, England
Height	1.83m
Date of Birth	07/11/78
Weight	75kg

At only 18 years of age he is being called England's answer to German star Matthias Sammer, a comparision made by the national coach, Glenn Hoddle. He is receiving praise everywhere he goes and it seems he cannot put a foot wrong. He is a defender who has the ability to come forward and play just as comfortably in the middle or up-front.

He is strong, powerful and has an unbelievably cool head for someone of such little experience and knowledge of the game. He will become an England favourite, but how long can West Ham afford to hang onto such talent?

John Moncur

Midfielder

Place of Birth Stepney, England

Height 1.70m

Date of Birth 22/09/66

Weight 58kg

Former Tottenham and Swindon midfielder John struggled with injury once again for part of the 96/97 season, yet was able to help the West Ham survival cause with some rousing performances in the middle of the park.

Chirpy chappy John is a typical West Ham player, able to pass to perfection and with plenty of skill and quality in most of what he does.

A real fans' favourite, he has fought for his place in the West Ham midfield which is full of top players such as Bishop, Hughes, Lomas and Williamson, all vying for those central midfield places.

Player of the Season

Julian Dicks

Defender

Place of Birth Bristol, England

Height 1.70m

Date of Birth 08/08/68

Weight 73kg

Once again Julian was quite magnificent for the Hammers and has proved himself to be the best uncapped player in English football.

The shaven haired left-back inspired his team to survival with some outstanding performances; his goalscoring tally was second to none – he finished top scorer for West Ham.

Reaching cult status with the fans obviously had a major part to play in Julian signing a new contract and the supporters know that he is a footballer who gives his absolute best and nothing less.

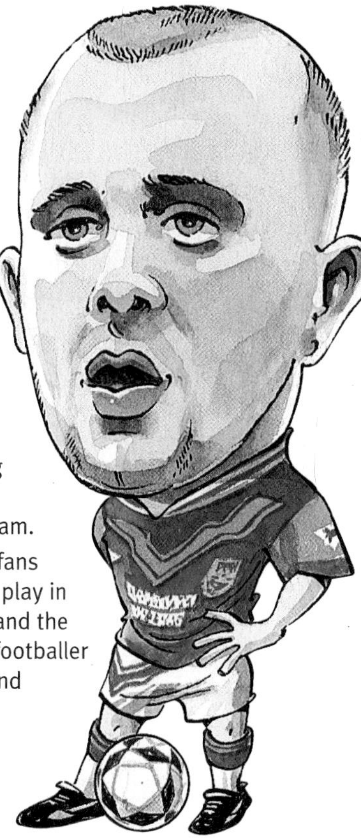

Paul Kitson

Striker

Place of Birth Murton, England

Height 1.77m

Date of Birth 09/01/71

Weight 67kg

He was signed at the same time as John Hartson but the spotlight on Paul was less intense as his price was much lower and he was known to be of Premiership standard.

His £2.3 million move to West Ham ended a horrible spell at Newcastle which saw him hardly ever getting a game. Redknapp saw that Paul had the ability and gave him the chance to show what he could do in the remaining 13 games of the season.

He managed to score some vital goals in the survival race and is now being looked at to score over 20 goals a season for the Hammers. He believes that he can achieve that goal in the 97/98 season.

West Ham United

STATS & FACTS

Club Details

Manager: Harry Redknapp

Assistant Manager: Frank Lampard

Captain: Julian Dicks

Colours: Home - Claret and Blue

Away - Ecru and Claret

Ground: Upton Park

Capacity: 26,014

CLUB HONOURS

FA Cup
Winners - 1964, 1975, 1980

European Cup Winners Cup - Winners 1965

What are their chances?

After much hope and promise for the 96/97 season, Hammers fans were left bitterly disappointed after enduring another relegation struggle.

Harry Redknapp eventually realised that he had to look at players that were actually going to want to play and not just take their money and run.

With players such as Dicks, Ferdinand and Hartson there is enough quality to see them stay up and gain a mid-table place; a good cup run is not out of the equation either.

PAST RECORD

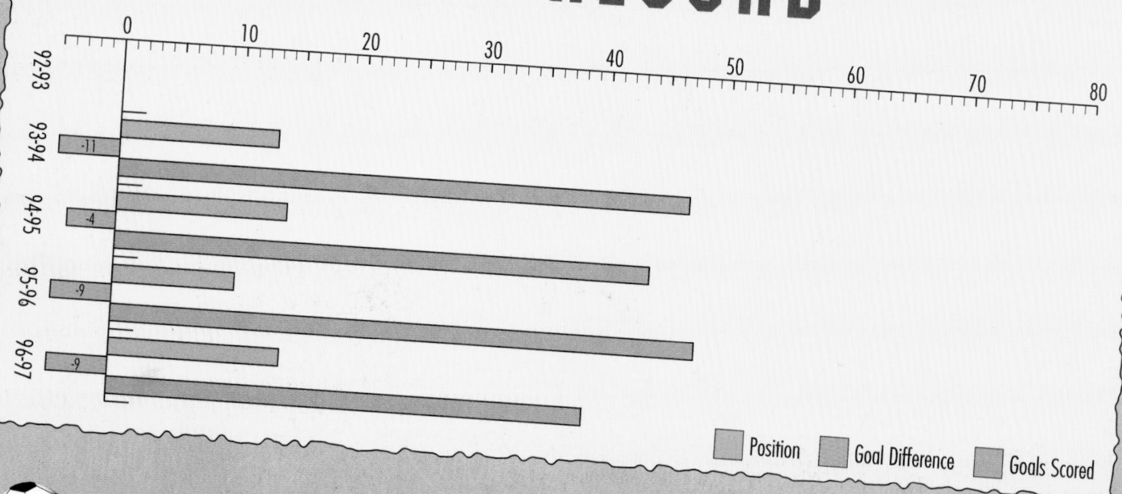

TITLE ODDS

80/1

ON AUGUST 9TH START OF SEASON

West Ham United

TEAM POSITIONS AND LINE-UP

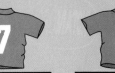

1 LUDEK MIKLOSKO	2 TIM BREACKER	3 JULIAN DICKS	4 STEVE POTTS	5 RICHARD HALL	6 DANNY WILLIAMSON
7 IAN BISHOP	8 MARC RIEPER	9 PAUL KITSON	10 JOHN HARTSON	11 STEVE LOMAS	12 KEITH ROWLAND
13 HUGO PORFIRIO	14 IAIN DOWIE	15	16 JOHN MONCUR	17 STAN LAZARIDIS	18
19	20	21 LES SEALEY	22	23	24 MICHAEL HUGHES
25	26 FRANK LAMPARD	27 RIO FERDINAND	28	29 EMMANUEL OMMOYIMINI	30
31	32	33	34	35	36

Vinnie Jones

Midfielder

Place of Birth	Watford, England
Height	1.83m
Date of Birth	05/01/65
Weight	75kg

The ever inspiring, ever controversial and ever charismatic midfielder would probably class the 96/97 season the best of his career. He can safely say that he played a major part in the success of Joe Kinnear's team.

Captaining the Crazy Gang is a tough job but there are few more capable of filling the role than Vinnie. Known as the typical hardman, his grit and determination are still evident yet he has shown the Premiership that he does possess skill and great vision.

Even though there is now some expertise to his game there is no doubt that he is not a player who you would like to wind up, he is still Vinnie Jones; THE hardman of English soccer.

Efan Ekoku

Striker

Place of Birth	Manchester, England
Height	1.85m
Date of Birth	08/06/67
Weight	76kg

Capped at international level, Nigerian Efan excelled in the 96/97 campaign and formed one of the most dangerous strike forces around with Marcus Gayle. The strong and pacey striker notched over 15 goals and proved himself a very tricky customer to defend against.

After a £1 million switch from Norwich a few seasons back, he was Wimbledon's record buy but for such an amount he now seems a bargain.

Despite rumours that he is about to move from Selhurst Park there has never been any doubt about his loyalty to the Dons or his gratitude to Joe Kinnear for giving him a chance in the Premiership.

Player to Watch

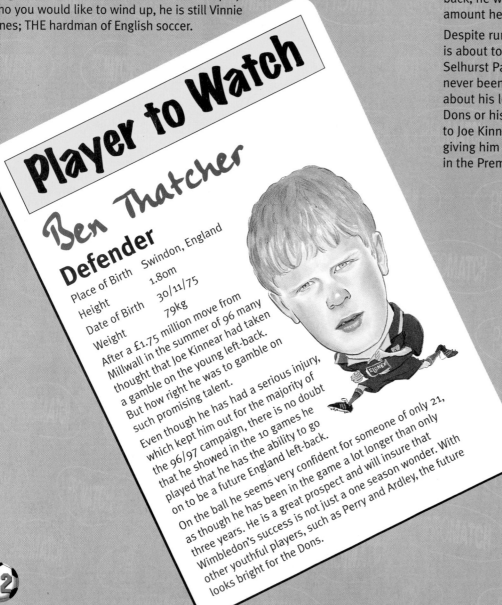

Ben Thatcher

Defender

Place of Birth	Swindon, England
Height	1.80m
Date of Birth	30/11/75
Weight	79kg

After a £1.75 million move from Millwall in the summer of 96 many thought that Joe Kinnear had taken a gamble on the young left-back. But how right he was to gamble on such promising talent.

Even though he has had a serious injury, which kept him out for the majority of the 96/97 campaign, there is no doubt that he showed in the 10 games he played that he has the ability to go on to be a future England left-back.

On the ball he seems very confident for someone of only 21, as though he has been in the game a lot longer than only three years. He is a great prospect and will insure that Wimbledon's success is not just a one season wonder. With other youthful players, such as Perry and Ardley, the future looks bright for the Dons.

Wimbledon

Oyvind Leonhardsen

Midfielder

Place of Birth	Rosenberg, Norway
Height	1.78m
Date of Birth	17/08/70
Weight	71kg

Tipped by many to be selected in the Premiership team of the season, he's richly deserved such recognition after another magnificent season for the Dons.

Since his move from Norway a few seasons ago he has always been regarded as the flair player in the Wimbledon side. Even though players around him now demonstrate more skilful play, Oyvind remains the man with the most ability.

He is rated at around £5 million and there has been interest from Italian sides yet he seems to be extremely happy at Wimbledon.

Player of the Season

Robbie Earle

Midfielder

Place of Birth	Newcastle-under-Lyme, England
Height	1.75m
Date of Birth	27/01/65
Weight	68kg

The best uncapped player in the Premiership; Robbie has astounded many by his inspirational and quite fantastic performances which helped Wimbledon achieve their success in the 96/97 season.

Now in his thirties, Robbie seems to be playing better than ever and the spirit that he gives to the team will have alerted Glenn Hoddle; with a need for a player of Robbie's type it is quite astonishing that he has not been selected for international honours.

With the end of his career not too far away a move into the managerial side of football is on the cards, after impressive interviews and radio commentaries, he is a player who certainly seems to know what he is talking about.

Marcus Gayle

Striker

Place of Birth	London, England
Height	1.88m
Date of Birth	27/09/70
Weight	82kg

He probably enjoyed the most remarkable resurgence of any player in 96/97. Following a season when he was lucky to get a game, being seen as one of the weaker squad members, Marcus suddenly became the most dangerous man in the Wimbledon side.

He won a battle with his confidence and enjoyed the best season of his life. Having shown what he can do he now hopes to prove he's not a one season wonder by going on to bigger and better things.

His pace and trickery, along with an awesome eye for goal, saw him finish top scorer for Wimbledon and the management now hope that they can keep him at Selhurst Park.

Wimbledon

STATS & FACTS

Club Details

Manager: Joe Kinnear

Assistant Manager: Terry Burton

Captain: Vinnie Jones

Colours: Home - Navy Blue and Yellow

Away - White and Black

Ground: Selhurst Park

Capacity: 26,309

CLUB HONOURS

FA Cup
Winners - 1988

What are their chances?

Unbelievable, incredible and astonishing are the words to describe Wimbledon's season of 96/97. With no disrespect to the Dons they could not in their wildest dreams have hoped to reach the heights they did, with success in the Premiership and both cup competitions.

With another season approaching, and pundits no longer so quick to put Wimbledon into the relegation bracket, they have the players in Gayle, Thatcher and Perry that can match the calibre of anyone else in the Premiership. There is no reason why they cannot build on the achievements of last season.

PAST RECORD

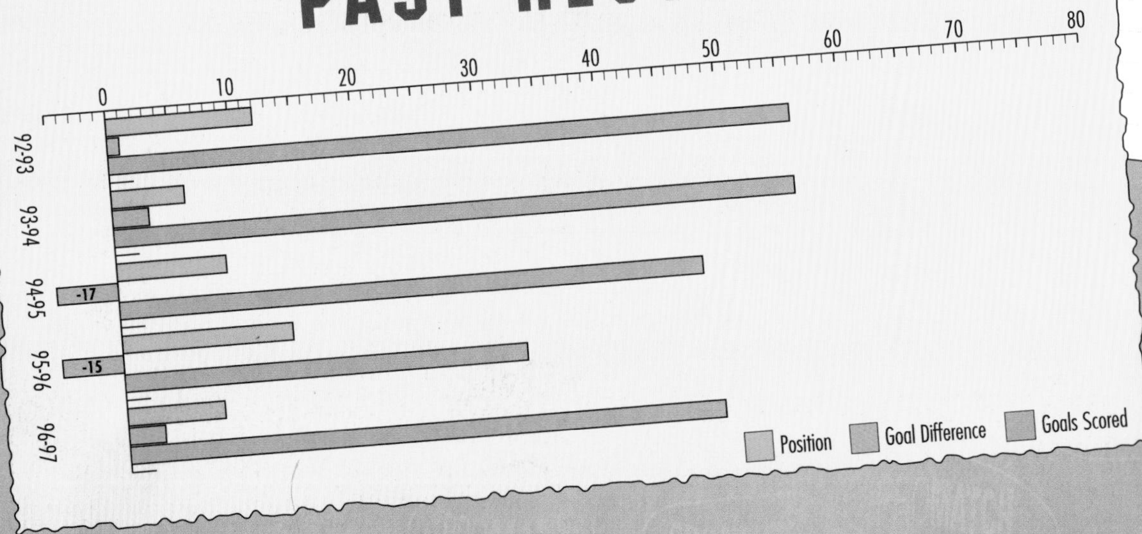

TITLE ODDS

50/1

ON AUGUST 9TH START OF SEASON

Wimbledon

TEAM POSITIONS AND LINE-UP

1	2	3	4	5	6
NEIL SULLIVAN	KENNY CUNNINGHAM	ALAN KIMBLE	VINNIE JONES	DEAN BLACKWELL	BEN THATCHER
7	8	9	10	11	12
ØYVIND LEONHARDSEN	ROBBIE EARLE	EFAN EKOKU	DEAN HOLDSWORTH	MARCUS GAYLE	CHRIS PERRY
13	14	15	16	17	18
PAUL HEALD	JON GOODMAN	ALAN REEVES		BRIAN MCALLISTER	NEIL ARDLEY
19	20	21	22	23	24
STEWART CASTLEDINE	MICK HARFORD	DUNCAN JUPP	ANDY CLARKE	JASON EVELL	PETER FEAR
25	26	27	28	29	30
ANDY PEARCE					
31	32	33	34	35	36

LIFE BEFORE THE

IN these days of wall-to-wall TV coverage, all-seater stadiums and Manchester United supremacy, it seems strange to recall a time in the distant past when these factors didn't dominate the English game. That distant time was... 1992.

Yes, 1992, the year SKY TV scooped the rights to exclusive live coverage of the English First Division, renamed the Premiership. It was also the year that Manchester United embarked on the 1992-93 season determined to break a 25-year sequence without an English championship.

They succeeded, winning the first of four Premiership titles. Yet while the rest of the Premiership may lag in United's slipstream a review of England's top division over its 109-year history gives United a total of 11 titles, well behind Liverpool's total of 18. The first Football League champions were Preston North End in 1889 and 1890 - they haven't won the trophy since, though they can claim to be the first winners, in 1889, of the elusive and coveted League and FA Cup double. The following year saw the first sighting of the modern day powers when Everton clinched the first of their nine championships. Liverpool, English football's major achievers, won their first title in 1901, quickly followed in the proceeding years by Newcastle and Manchester United.

Manchester United, Newcastle, Liverpool; nearly a century later, little has changed at the top of the English game. But the first team to dominate the Football League was Huddersfield Town, who won three successive championships from 1924 to 1926, a feat only equalled by Arsenal (1933-35) and Liverpool (1982-84). The English league isn't the best in the world but the fact that Championship hat tricks are so rare suggests that it's probably the hardest and most competitive.

Hard it certainly is, but over the years there have been champions of such skill and quality that they've stood out from the pack, a match for anything on the Continent. Herbert Chapman's Arsenal team which dominated the 1930s; the unfulfilled potential of the late 1950s pre-Munich Manchester United; the immortal Spurs Double team of 1961; the feared Leeds United sides of the late 1960s and early 1970s; the remorseless Liverpool teams of the 1970s and 1980s (the teams of 78-79 and 87-88 were standouts).

But it's a democratic league, not the exclusive preserve of the big boys;

PREMIERSHIP

a glance at the 23 clubs who've won league titles reveals unlikely triumphs for Nottingham Forest in 1978, Derby County in 1972, way back to Ipswich Town in 1962 (having been promoted the previous year).

Despite these shocks the power base of English football is established in the North West of England. From Preston in 1889 to Manchester United in 1997, the region has produced a total of 47 champions. Yet anyone looking for winners from London has to search long and hard. Arsenal may be third on the all-time list with 10 wins but the capital has produced only three other winners - Tottenham (1951 and 1961) and Chelsea (1955). Whether this can be explained by the various distractions of the capital's nightlife or the intense demands caused by the proliferation of London derbies is one of the ongoing debates in English football.

Arsenal's most famous title triumph occurred in 1989, breaking Liverpool's era of dominance. The Merseyside club's roll of modern success began in 1973 - over the next 17 years they won a further 10 titles, spearheaded by a succession of world class forwards - Keegan, Dalglish, Rush, Beardsley and Barnes. The introduction of three points for a win in 1981-82 only served to emphasise that Liverpool won more games than anyone else.

In the 1980s the Championship virtually resided on Merseyside - when Liverpool didn't win it, Everton (1985 and 87) did. Only Aston Villa (1981) and Arsenal, famously, in 1989 stemmed the Mersey flow. In the final game of the 88-89 season, Arsenal went to Anfield needing to win by two goals to clinch the title and prevent Liverpool achieving a second League and FA Cup double. A minute into injury time, the Gunners lead by a goal.

Then Arsenal's Michael Thomas broke into the Liverpool penalty area with only the goalkeeper to beat. Forty-two thousand spectators and a nationwide television audience held its breath. Thomas lifted the ball over Bruce Grobelaar. Two-nil! Ninety seconds later Arsenal were, incredibly, League champions.

Liverpool's aura of invincibility was shattered - they'd lost before but never had they thrown away such an unassailable position. Anfield's last title was in 1990 and we now live in the Old Trafford years.

But no-one stays on top forever. Even if you support Ipswich Town or Portsmouth (winners in 1949 and 50) your time may come. It's bound to, in the Premiership, the world's most competitive league.

Arsenal

RONNIE PARKS, 12

WILL ARSENAL FULFIL LAST SEASON'S POTENTIAL?

"With Bergkamp and Wright anything is possible. But we've got to stop losing so many games at Highbury. If we'd beaten Liverpool and Man United there last season we'd have won the League."

Aston Villa

NICK HIGGS, 11

ARE VILLA DESTINED TO REMAIN JUST A GOOD CUP SIDE?

"Unless Roy Keane and Schmeichel get injured, I can't see anyone beating Man United over a season but Villa have the potential to be second best. Now Dwight Yorke is partnering Stan Collymore we'll score more. Milosevic won't do. He scores one great goal a season then misses sitters."

Barnsley

PAUL BURNS, 12

BARNSLEY ARE ONLY A SMALL CLUB. HAVE THEY THE RESOURCES TO STAY UP?

"Blackburn were a small club when they got promoted and look what they did. And it's not all about money. Blackburn only had one great player in Alan Shearer, the rest were average. We just need to make one good buy and we can do as well as anyone. We certainly won't go down."

Bolton

JIM BLACKHURST, 10

ARE BOLTON GOING STRAIGHT BACK DOWN AGAIN LIKE THEY DID IN 95/96?

"Not this time. The players know what to expect this time. We'll stay up, no problem. Nathan Blake will frighten the life out of slow, square defences 'cos he's the quickest player in England."

Blackburn Rovers

HELEN ROBERTS, 13

WAS BLACKBURN'S 1995 TITLE SUCCESS A ONE-SEASON WONDER?

"Yes. We lost Dalglish which was bad but then losing Shearer was even worse. The remaining players haven't got any better apart from Colin Hendry and he can't do it on his own. Hopefully Roy Hodgson will attract top players but I'm not optimistic."

Chelsea

SHELLEY CARTER, 11

IS THIS FINALLY CHELSEA'S YEAR FOR THE PREMIERSHIP?

"Only if we play every game like a cup tie, then we'll walk it. But all the players, even the skillful ones, need to battle like Mark Hughes. Too many of them fall asleep during normal League games. Ruud Gullit's great but he should tell our players that they have to perform in every game."

Derby County

LYNN McGARRIGLE, 14

EVERYONE THOUGHT DERBY WOULD BE RELEGATED. WHY DID THEY SURVIVE?

"Because of Jim Smith. He knows everything about managing teams with no money and all the players respect him. This season we're in our new stadium which will inspire the players to do even better. I think we'll be top ten."

Everton

WINONA WILLIAMS, 13

WHO WAS TO BLAME FOR EVERTON'S TERRIBLE SEASON?

"Joe Royle. If he'd have stayed we'd have gone down. He got rid of Kanchelskis, our best player, and brought in First Division rubbish. But in three years, when we move to our 60,000 stadium, we'll be number one again."

Leeds United

NICK JOHN, 12

LEEDS WERE SO BORING LAST SEASON THEY WEREN'T WORTH GETTING OUT OF BED TO WATCH. TRUE OR FALSE?

"Yes we were dull but we didn't go down. George Graham made us hard to beat. Now George's got to give Tony Yeboah a kick up the backside. He's had a season off, now we need his goals. Oh yeah, and Ian Rush just won't do, he's past it."

Leicester City

MARK BUTCHER, 14

HOW WILL LEICESTER DO IN EUROPE?

"If we draw an Italian side we're out. But we can beat any side from any other country at Filbert Street. Then we'd just have to hassle them away from home, like we did to Middlesbrough in the Coca-Cola Cup final."

Fans' Opinions

Liverpool

JOHNNY HUMPHREYS, 13

LIVERPOOL UNDERACHIEVED AGAIN LAST SEASON. CAN THEY DO BETTER?

"Yes. If we get rid of James, Barnes and Redknapp. We need players who care for the club and aren't worried about getting their kit dirty in case it looks bad in photos. I'd rather our players were on the back pages of newspapers celebrating victories rather than on the front pages with the Spice Girls."

Manchester United

DAVE COLLINS, 11

MAN UNITED CAN BUY ALMOST ANY PLAYER SO WHO WOULD YOU LIKE TO SEE AT OLD TRAFFORD?

"Boksic from Juventus. He did us in Europe last season. He's worth four Andy Coles. If we had Boksic the League would be over by Christmas. Alan Shearer would be good as well but that's not going to happen. To be honest, even if Fergie doesn't buy anyone we'll win the League – again."

Sheffield Wednesday

JEZ STANFIELD, 14

ARE WEDNESDAY AN ORDINARY SIDE FLATTERED BY LAST SEASON'S LEAGUE POSITION?

"No."

CAN YOU ELABORATE?

"Just 'cos we've no high-profile players doesn't mean we're ordinary. We battle for each other and teams like Liverpool could learn from our attitude. As far as skill goes, Benito Carbone is as good as Zola."

Newcastle United

NEIL RAINE, 14

WILL NEWCASTLE'S DEFENCE EVER BE STRONG ENOUGH TO SUSTAIN A TITLE CHALLENGE?

"Probably not. But we score so many goals it shouldn't be a problem. If Shearer stays fit all season then we can win the League, it won't matter how many goals we let in. If Blackburn can win the League with Shearer then we certainly can."

Tottenham Hotspur

EDDIE LUND, 14

ARE SPURS MORE CONCERNED ABOUT THEIR FINANCES OR ON THE PITCH SUCCESS?

"Finances. Alan Sugar should dip into his pockets and buy back Jurgen Klinsmann. If not, he should buy two or three other German internationals. They'd make Spurs tough to beat 'cos we're a soft touch at the moment."

West Ham United

KEELY GILES, 13

WEST HAM BEAT THE DROP ONCE AGAIN SO ARE YOU A HAPPY HAMMER?

"Yes. Every time we avoid relegation it's a success. This season we should do better with Hartson and Kitson up front. Those two saved us last year. But I'd like to have a good cup run for once. It might cheer up Harry Redknapp."

Southampton

GABE RAPPINI, 14

IS MATT LE TISSIER STILL VITAL TO SOUTHAMPTON?

"My friends will kill me but Matt hasn't done it for a couple of seasons now. Everyone remembers the great goal against Newcastle last season but that was about it. We should cash in – we could still get six or seven million for him. Maybe Chelsea are still interested."

Wimbledon

BILLY WELSH, 14

WIMBLEDON FELL AWAY BADLY AT THE END OF LAST SEASON. CAN THEY SUSTAIN TOP FORM FOR THE WHOLE OF THE SEASON?

"We could easily finish top three but we'd have to get knocked out of the cups early on. Last season the players were exhausted by March. All the teams who did well in both the cups - Leicester and Middlesbrough as well - struggled at the end of the season. We had too many games and too few players."

Coventry

STEVE ASHCROFT, 10

IF RON ATKINSON HAD STAYED AS MANAGER, WOULD YOU HAVE GONE DOWN?

"Definitely. Big Ron's been a great manager at other clubs, but he's no good here. Gordon Strachan had the respect of the players who wanted to play for him. Ron Atkinson should stay on television making those 'funny' comments of his."

Crystal Palace

KAREN EVANS, 12

PALACE HAVE BEEN RELEGATED TWICE IN THE 90S. WILL THEY GO DOWN AGAIN THIS YEAR?

"Who knows? We just scraped into the Premiership but sometimes that's a good thing. Derby and Leicester did better than Sunderland last season and they'd walked the First Division title. We'll be tough to beat at Selhurst Park but I think we could get a few hidings away from home."

SCOTTISH PREMIER LEAGUE

Once again Rangers became champions of the Scottish League and showed their absolute dominance in the top flight, north of the border.

Yet they failed again to make a name for themselves in the Champions League, though equalling Celtic's record of nine successive Scottish titles was some consolation. Walter Smith was reluctant to use the millions that he had readily available nor was he keen to use players from the youth side, instead he kept faith with much of the squad who won the title the previous year. Brian Laudrup was again quite outstanding and with Paul Gascoigne out for long periods he found himself as the central playmaker. After winning the title in such comfortable fashion, they will again be looking to the European Cup for more glory, but can Walter Smith succeed at another go?

Celtic were always thought of as Rangers' major challengers but failed to live up to their pre-season hype. Players such as Di Canio and Cadete flourished and almost looked, at times, as though the League was far too easy for them yet the rest of the team let them down on occasions and a season of much promise delivered nothing but that second spot which they are finding uncomfortably comfortable. Celtic must look forward to their youth system if they can and, as much as they won't like it, to succeed they must follow the way in which Rangers have applied themselves.

Dundee United had an astonishing season. After being promoted they became one of the hardest teams to beat in Scotland, finished third and claimed a European place.

St. Johnstone were one of the most consistent teams in the whole of Britain and this form saw them automatically promoted six games before the end of the season. They look as though they have the talent to show a few teams that they are not going straight back down.

After such a good season a few years ago, Raith Rovers were doomed to the drop and they can look back on a dismal year which they'll be glad is over.

With many saying the Scottish League is dominated by the Glasgow clubs, there are signs that other sides are starting to attract quality players and that, hopefully, the coming season will be a wider and closer race than of late.

Fans' Opinions

Hearts

JOHNATHON HENRY, 13

WITH GLASGOW CLUBS LOOKING INVINCIBLE DO YOU THINK THAT A CLUB LIKE YOURS, IN EDINBURGH, WILL EVER BE ABLE TO CHALLENGE THE LIKES OF RANGERS AND CELTIC?

"I do, I think the next season is the one when it's going to happen. It has gone on too long and we now have the basis to become one of the biggest teams in Scotland. Players from abroad have come to us, from Italy and France, so it's possible that we will be able to get some more of the top players in the world to play for us. We will challenge for the League this year."

Motherwell

DAVID WESTLAKE, 12

AFTER THAT NAILBITING FINISH WITH AIRDRIE IN THE PLAYOFFS DO YOU THINK THAT YOU WILL BOUNCE BACK FROM THAT?

"We had a look at what it would be like to go down into the First Division and we really did not like the look of it! We will certainly make changes in the summer and when those changes are made then I can see us pushing for one of those European places at the end of the season."

Kilmarnock

ALAN HARDING, 12

THAT UP AND DOWN SEASON CERTAINLY MADE YOU SMILE ESPECIALLY WINNING THE CUP?

"It was fantastic, just great, the atmosphere and everything, yet to be honest I got a better buzz out of beating Rangers at Ibrox. To me that is my highlight of the season."

WHAT ABOUT PAUL WRIGHT, MANY SAY THAT HE IS ON HIS WAY OUT?

"I hope not after keeping us up and scoring some brilliant goals. I don't want to see him go as I think he is one of the best strikers in the Scottish game."

Celtic

ADAM GREGAN, 11

ANOTHER SEASON AND YOU FINISH BEHIND YOUR ARCH RIVALS, WHAT DO YOU THINK HAS TO BE DONE TO CHANGE IT ?

"We've got to beat Rangers in the Old Firm games. If we'd have done that last season, we'd have won the League. But when we play Rangers, the referee's always on their side."

WHAT SORT OF PLAYERS WOULD YOU LIKE TO SEE COME IN?

"With Paul McStay now going we need a playmaker, Kinkladze or even Gazza. I would love to see Gazza in a hoops shirt!"

Hibernian

GARY LONGMAN, 12

AFTER JUST AVOIDING THE DROP AND NOT HAVING MUCH TO SHOUT ABOUT LAST SEASON, WHO WOULD YOU LIKE TO SEE COME IN TO MAKE A DIFFERENCE AT HIBERNIAN?

"First of all we have to keep Darren Jackson, he has shown that for his club and country he is probably the best Scottish striker playing in Scotland. I would like to see us buy a strong midfielder and defender, someone like Richard Gough."

WHAT ABOUT THE COMING SEASON?

"To be honest if we do not bring in anyone new then it is going to be another struggle. I just hope that we can finish above Hearts, that is my aim for this season."

St. Johnstone

PAUL McCAULEY, 12

FIRST THINGS FIRST, DO YOU THINK YOU CAN STAY UP?

"Honestly, I think it is going to be tough, everyone is saying that we can go and do what Dundee United have gone and done but we do not have the players or the manager to get a place in Europe."

SO YOU ARE NOT OPTIMISTIC. WHAT ABOUT THE CONFIDENCE THE PLAYERS WILL HAVE FROM THE PROMOTION SEASON?

"Don't get me wrong, we had a magnificent season last year and it is the best year I have ever seen, but I think that other clubs are going to buy big whereas we will have to make do with what we have."

Dundee United

DAVID LUCAS, 13

WITH SUCH A FANTASTIC SEASON BEHIND YOU WHAT DO YOU THINK OF YOUR CHANCES FOR THE COMING YEAR?

"We can win the UEFA Cup. Why not? Everyone thought that we would go straight back down and look at us, we finished above Aberdeen and the Edinburgh clubs and got that European spot."

THAT IS A BIT OPTIMISTIC ISN'T IT?

"I suppose but if we keep our team, have good old Maurice Malpas fit and get some players in from Europe, like the Glasgow teams have done, then you never know."

Dunfermline

STEVE TROLLOPE, 14

MANY SAY THAT DUNFERMLINE WERE ONE OF THE YO-YO CLUBS IN THE LEAGUE BUT HOW DO YOU ANSWER THOSE CRITICS NOW AFTER HAVING ONE OF THE BEST SEASONS FOR YEARS?

"I never expected us to stay up and certainly not to finish midway in the league. It has on occasions been aggravating because there have been times when we have been able to move even higher up the League and we did not take that chance."

WHO IS YOUR PLAYER OF THE SEASON AND YOUR PLAYER TO WATCH OUT FOR?

"Gerry Britton is the man to watch and my player of the year; he is tall, strong and knows how to put the ball in the back of the net."

Rangers

JAMES FARINGDON, 12

YOU MUST OBVIOUSLY BE DELIGHTED WITH THE SEASON AS A WHOLE BUT DO YOU NOT FEEL THAT YOU ARE BEING LET DOWN BY THE CLUB'S BAD PERFORMANCES IN EUROPE?

"We won the League again and you cannot ask more from a team but you are right that we are giving Scotland bad representation in Europe. I think that the only way it will change is if we get some new ideas in."

SO YOU THINK WALTER SMITH SHOULD GO?

"I want to see someone like Arsene Wenger come in and go alongside Walter, but the most important thing is we finish above Celtic!"

Aberdeen

SEAN McGARRIGLE, 12

ALWAYS THOUGHT OF AS THE THIRD TEAM IN SCOTLAND, IT SEEMS NOW ABERDEEN ARE NOT EVEN MANAGING THIRD SPOT. WHAT IS GOING ON AT PITTODRIE?

"Come on though, we haven't got a chance! The Glasgow teams have got all the money and the best players and the rest of us are left with the rest. It isn't fair and something should be done!"

BUT WHAT?

"Teams should have a limited amount of money to spend and also should have a certain number of players that were born in their area to play for that team; I know so many people who support Rangers and Celtic who live around me and it is so silly, just because they are the big teams!"

Brian Irvine

Defender

Place of Birth Belshill, Scotland   Height 1.84m
Date of Birth 24/05/65   Weight 86kg

Now in his eleventh season at Pittodrie he is still a firm favourite with the crowd and is one of the most experienced defenders in Scotland.

At the age of 32 he does not seem as though he has lost his vision or strength and the experience that he has gained through the years has obviously proven to be important considering his performances in the last few seasons.

Having played for the national side nine times in his career, he has stressed that he would love to try and perform on the international scene again and help Scotland to the World Cup finals in France.

Antoine Koumbuare

Defender

Place of Birth France
Height 1.81m
Date of Birth 16/11/63
Weight 81kg

When arriving for a nominal fee during the 95/96 season, Aberdeen fans looked forward to seeing what the Frenchman could do in helping to seal a leaky defence that has often been Aberdeen's downfall.

A tall and inspiring player, who leads the pack with confidence and ability, he also has a very hard shot and many top teams in Scotland have fallen to Antoine's powerful free-kicks.

He's now being looked at by many teams in the Scottish and English Premiership so it looks as though there could be a rosy future for him.

Dean Windass

Striker

Place of Birth Hull, England Height 1.76m

Date of Birth 01/04/69 Weight 79kg

With the decline of his former club, Hull City, it was time for Dean to move on to a better standard of football. With offers from many clubs it was the chance of a fresh challenge in Scotland that proved most attractive.

An attacking midfielder turned forward he is one of the flair players that they have in their ranks. His vital passes have led to many a goal for Booth and Dodds.

He has a strong belief that there are the players at Pittodrie with the ability to challenge Celtic and Rangers for the title in the near future.

Scott Booth

Striker

Place of Birth Aberdeen, Scotland

Height 1.74m

Date of Birth 16/12/71

Weight 77kg

At the age of 25, Scott isn't mentioned as much now. Earlier in his career many felt he had a great future in the game. Yet he still has a high reputation in the Scottish Premier Division and with his strike partner, Billy Dodds, the goals have continued to flow over the years.

During the 96/97 season there were proposed moves to Blackburn or Bolton but Scott felt that it was not the right time for him to move. He felt playing in Scotland would enhance his chances of increasing his 13 cap total for his country as the 1998 World Cup approaches.

Alan Stubbs

Defender

Place of Birth	Kirkby, England	Height	1.87m
Date of Birth	06/10/71	Weight	86kg

When the central defender finally decided to move from Bolton Wanderers in a deal worth in the region of £3.5 million, he was bought to lead a championship challenge against Celtic's intense rivals, Rangers. But his presence failed to prevent Rangers winning a record-equalling ninth consecutive title.

At the time he broke Celtic's transfer record and for a defender it was an awful lot of money to pay, yet there is no doubt about his quality and his defending capabilities.

He proved in his first season what a difference he can make, despite suffering from injuries. His growing confidence on the ball may yet convince Glenn Hoddle to go north of the border to watch Celtic's captain.

Paul McStay

Midfielder

Place of Birth	Hamilton, Scotland	Height	1.78m
Date of Birth	22/10/64	Weight	77kg

After playing at Celtic for over ten years, the old war-horse is still able to command a first team place and despite suffering from injuries during 96/97, when he did get back towards the end of the season he showed his undoubted quality.

A Celtic team would not seem the same without Paul, who has given so much to the superhoops, and has rejected moves to Italy in the past.

An ever-present in the Scottish squad, he will no doubt end up taking a job in football management; his leadership and captaincy skills make him a natural for such a role when he ends his playing career.

Jorge Cadete

Striker

Place of Birth Mozambique Height 1.84m

Date of Birth 27/08/68 Weight 81kg

With Van Hooijdonk gone to Nottingham Forest the fans have not even whispered the Dutchman's name due to the unbelievable form of the Portuguese ace who finished amongst the top scorers in the Premiership.

When arriving, initially on loan, from Sporting Lisbon he impressed immediately and convinced the then manager Tommy Burns that Jorge's future belonged at Celtic. He soon joined the Parkhead club in a multi-million pound deal.

With over 20 goals last season he has become a firm favourite with the fans; his stylish long hair and cosmopolitan style may have made him a hit with the female fans but if he can help Celtic to a long-awaited title, he will be loved by all!

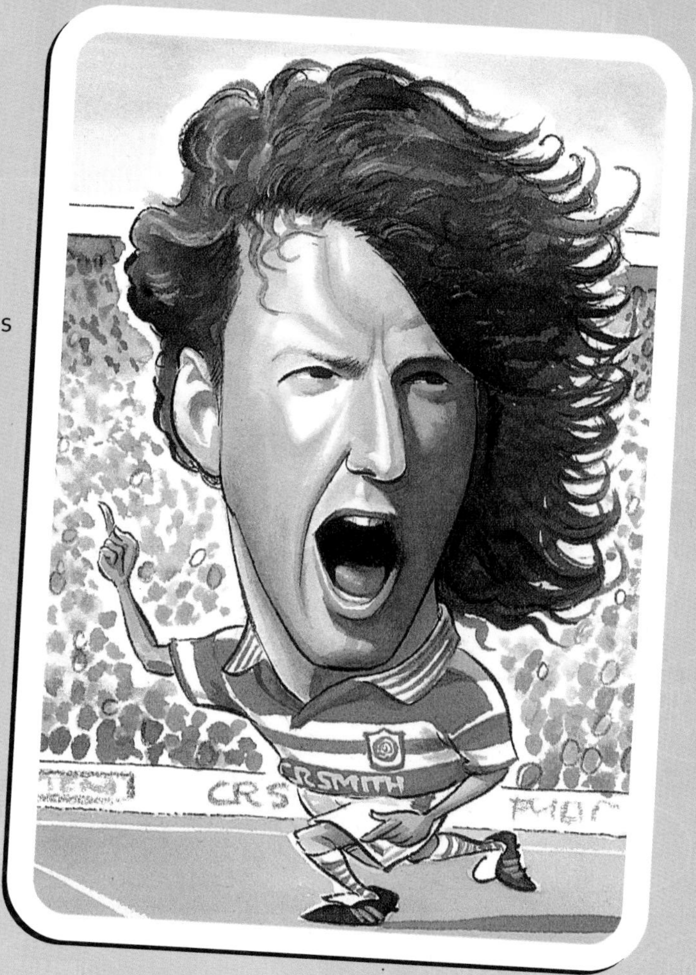

Celtic

Paulo Di Canio

Midfielder

Place of Birth Rome, Italy

Height 1.79m

Date of Birth 09/07/68

Weight 76kg

After tiring of sitting on the sidelines at Milan, Paulo was coolly snapped up by Tommy Burns for £1.5 million where he had a magnificent first season in the Premier Division.

His nimble feet, in his trademark white boots, have made him a cult figure and he's regarded as Celtic's 'Laudrup' though Old Firm fans will dispute long and hard over who is the best!

His fiery temperament and strong desire to win saw him get into disciplinary trouble yet his character and passion are typically Italian and, in the hurry and bustle of the Scottish game, it is no wonder that his skills and temperament don't always agree with the opposition.

Andy Goram

Goalkeeper

Place of Birth Bury, England   Height 1.84m

Date of Birth 13/04/64   Weight 82kg

Probably regarded as one of the most consistent goalkeepers to appear in the Scottish Premier Division, Andy has helped Rangers dominate football in Scotland over the past five seasons.

A veteran at 33, yet still undisputed as the number one at Ibrox. On the international scene he is one of the only players in the Rangers side who has kept his place during their reign at the top of the league.

A return to the English Premiership has often been rumoured and, with his career starting off at Oldham Athletic, it was likely but now, at his age, it seems as though he will remain at Rangers where he will stake his claim to be included in the Ibrox hall of fame.

Jorg Albertz

Midfielder

Place of Birth Germany   Height 1.78m

Date of Birth 29/01/71   Weight 77kg

What a hit the German has become, his determination and skill combined have made the unknown £4 million man an instant success with the Rangers faithful.

Jorg has certainly weighed in with his share of goals, especially from set-pieces where a free-kick from outside the area is equally as dangerous as a penalty kick; the power in his shot is frighteningly strong.

The 'German bomber' - in the phraseology of the Scottish press - is still only 26 and is beginning to catch the eye of Berti Vogts. He could easily become the man to take over the role of Andy Moller whose career may soon be coming to an end.

Paul Gascoigne

Midfielder

Place of Birth	Gateshead, England	Height	1.78m
Date of Birth	27/05/67	Weight	83kg

There is not much more that can be said about 'Gazza' after years of endless publicity, controversy and of course giving so much pleasure with his phenomenal skill and vision.

The past season has seen Paul struggle with injury but when available he is, without doubt, the best player in Scotland and can turn a match with a piece of inspiration.

As Paul hits the 30 mark he does not seem bothered: 'I will not let my age restrict me and as long as I can do my best, I feel that I am just as fit as when I was a young lad!'

Brian Laudrup

Striker

Place of Birth	Vienna, Austria
Height	1.82m
Date of Birth	22/02/69
Weight	82kg

Until Brian's arrival three seasons ago, Glasgow fans had never really experienced the wonders of a true top class continental player. His arrival changed that.

His pace and skill can destroy teams, allowing him to tear defences apart. He scored over 20 goals last season, as well as setting up countless attacks. These qualities gave him the honour of being the only Scottish league footballer to be selected in the world's top 50 players.

On his return to the Danish set-up after a dispute with the manager, he and his brother, Michael, have re-formed their partnership and hope to help the country to the World Cup in France.

Gilles Rousset

Goalkeeper

Place of Birth	Hyeres, France	Height	1.86m
Date of Birth	22/08/63	Weight	98kg

The giant French goalkeeper has become a huge favourite with the fans since his move from French club Sochaux a couple of seasons ago.

Having played for his country on two occasions, it was obviously quite a coup for Hearts to be able to tempt Gilles to come and help them stop conceding goals; goals which have prevented them challenging Rangers and Celtic.

Even though he will be remembered for his embarrassing performance in the 1995 Scottish Cup final, most Hearts fans will tell you that he is one of the best keepers that they have seen for years.

Gary Locke

Defender

Place of Birth	Edinburgh, Scotland	Height	1.75m
Date of Birth	16/06/75	Weight	71kg

At only 21 he was the youngest club captain in Scotland and that obviously says a lot about the young Scotsman's potential.

He is committed to the Hearts cause of challenging for honours and is defiantly against moving on to any of the bigger clubs in Scotland.

He has shown great character after being stretchered off when he was injured in the 95 Cup final. Many fans were saddened to see such an enthusiastic player being deprived of glory on his biggest day.

Pasquale Bruno

Defender

Place of Birth Lecce, Italy Height 1.81m

Date of Birth 19/06/62 Weight 82kg

When signed for a nominal fee from Italian giants Torino many fans in Scotland had to look twice at an Italian moving across the channel into the Scottish league.

He has shown that he has all the qualities of a continental defender: timing, patience and wonderful vision and, of course, that sly attitude that Italian players are born with.

His clubs include Fiorentina and Juventus, giving him superb credentials, and he is hoping that by finishing his career at Hearts he can also help them to win major trophies.

Hearts

John Robertson

Striker

Place of Birth Edinburgh, Scotland

Height 1.75m

Date of Birth 02/10/64

Weight 81kg

Over the last ten years whenever a goal is scored for Hearts one automatically thinks of John Robertson.

Most seasons he finishes top scorer for the club that he loves but he has never really been considered for his country despite such an impressive goalscoring record. At 33 it looks doubtful that he will ever be given a real chance at international level.

He has the knack of always being in the right place at the right time and, with his goalscoring record, it is easy to see why he is one of the most dangerous marksmen in the Premier Division.

Dundee United

Gary McSwegan

Striker

Place of Birth Glasgow, Scotland Height 1.75m
Date of Birth 03/10/74 Weight 74kg

Having been brought up through the ranks at Glasgow Rangers he was not going to play second fiddle to Ally McCoist. He had a spell with Notts County but was then returned to Scotland where he has had an enjoyable spell with Dundee United.

Gary's not always in the starting line-up but he is a player with plenty of talent and has the makings of a top striker.

Now approaching the peak of his career, he will be hoping that in the coming season he can show Rangers what they missed.

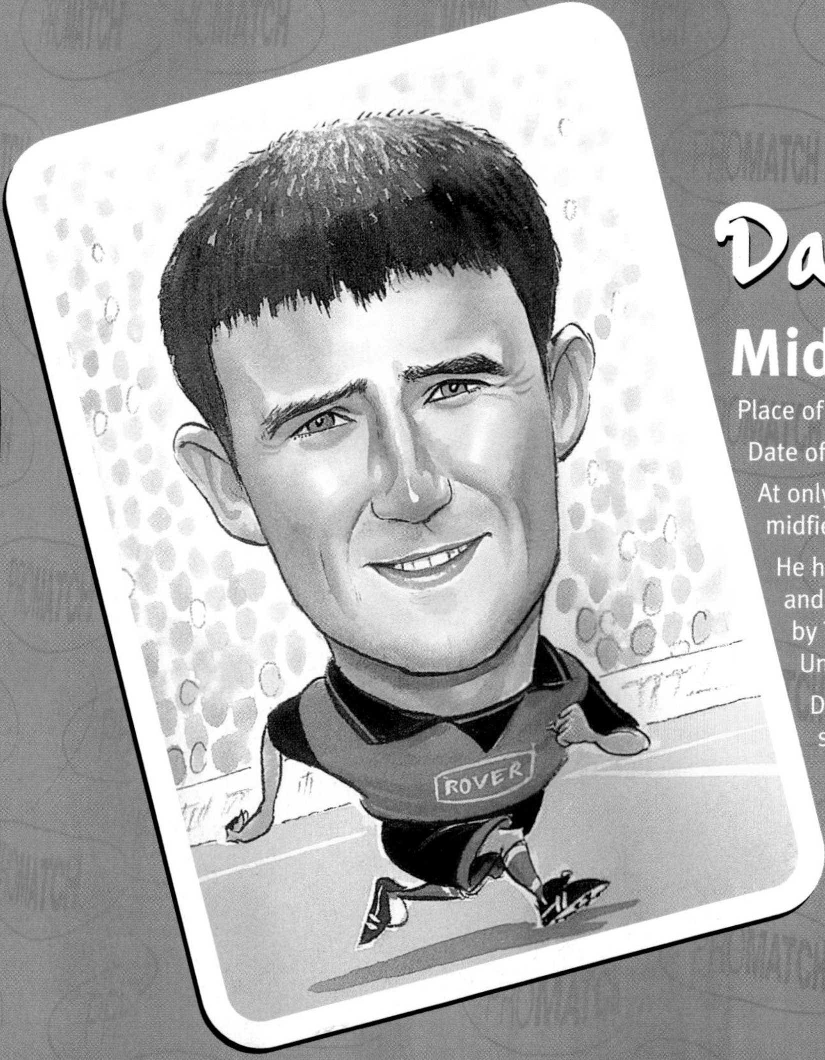

David Hannah

Midfielder

Place of Birth Coatbridge, Scotland Height 1.78m
Date of Birth 04/08/74 Weight 80kg

At only 22 he is said to be one of the most versatile midfielders around and is tipped for a great future.

He has been tracked by many clubs around Britain and has been watched since he was an 18 year-old by Tottenham Hotspur, so there is no doubt that United will struggle to keep him.

David and his team-mates have enjoyed a very successful season after promotion and it's to be hoped that wherever he is next year he can again enjoy success.

Hibernian

Darren Jackson

Striker

Place of Birth Edinburgh, Scotland

Height 1.80m

Date of Birth 25/07/66

Weight 75kg

After a proposed move to Celtic fell through the former Newcastle and Dundee United man has again shown that he is one of the hottest properties in Scottish football.

Now a Scottish international he would love to be part of the squad that could take Scotland to France. If they do qualify there is nothing that he would like better than to play in the World Cup finals.

His pace and ability to hold the ball up are his main attributes, making him one of the best all-round strikers in the Scottish game.

Pat McGinlay

Midfielder

Place of Birth Glasgow, Scotland

Height 1.78m

Date of Birth 30/05/67

Weight 72kg

Although one of the top goalscoring midfielders in the Scottish Premiership, Pat did not have one of his best years in 96/97 but is still one of the most talented players at Easter Road.

Signed from Celtic for £400,000, his value will probably have doubled now he's established himself as one of the top goalscoring midfielders in Scotland.

He is sometimes over-passionate in his approach but he is worshipped by the Hibernian faithful and will be remembered for a long time.

Kilmarnock

Paul Wright

Striker

Place of Birth East Kilbride, Scotland

Height 1.78m

Date of Birth 17/08/67

Weight 72kg

Bought for £340,000 a few seasons ago, he has been a huge success at Kilmarnock and was a major factor in his team's battle to stay in the top flight.

Having had spells for Hibernian and Queens Park Rangers in the past, he seems to have fitted in nicely at Rugby Park.

A quality player with a great first touch and the ability to score some outstanding goals, notably his winning goal in the Scottish Cup Final.

Motherwell

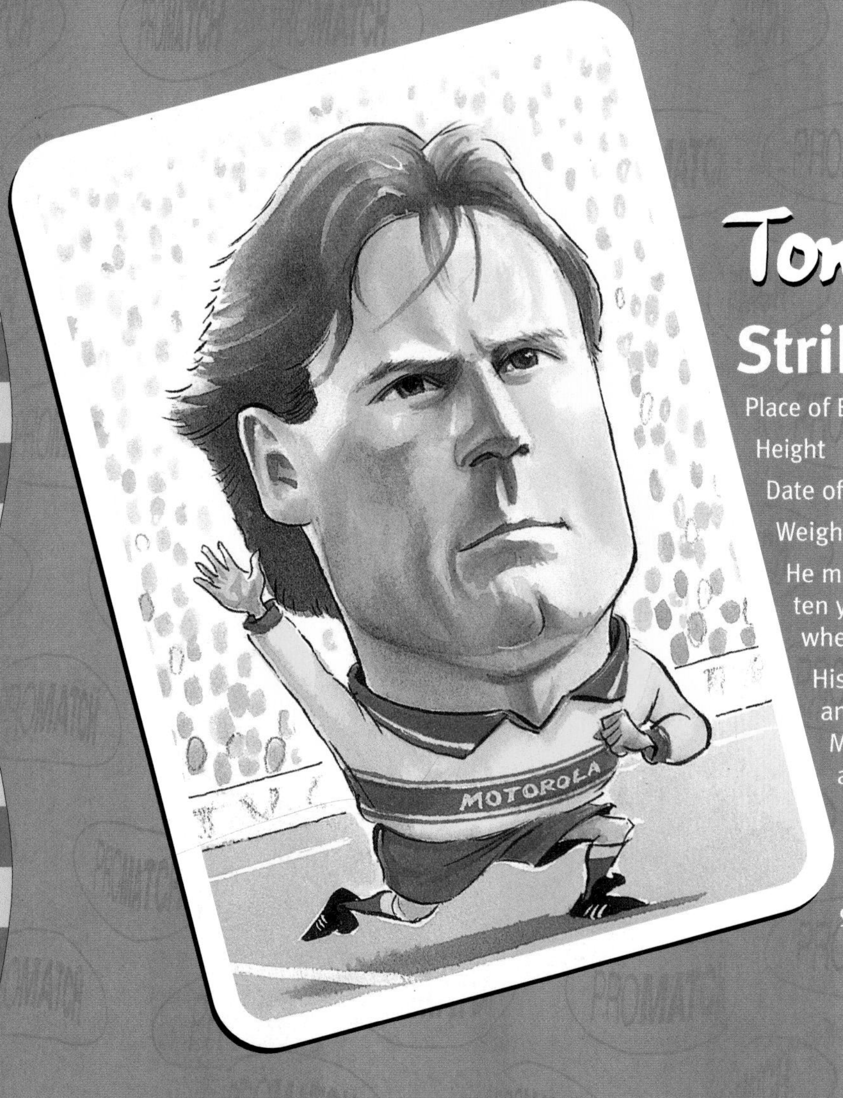

Tommy Coyne

Striker

Place of Birth Glasgow, Scotland

Height 1.79m

Date of Birth 14/11/62

Weight 74kg

He made a name for himself when playing for Dundee United ten years ago and was then brought to the English game where he had a tremendous record at Tranmere Rovers.

His time at Tranmere was successful yet he had to leave and move back to Scotland for personal reasons; Motherwell were more than happy to take him on board and he has scored some vital goals.

The Eire International is hoping that, in what maybe be his last season, he can score enough goals to make sure Motherwell don't struggle like they did in the 96/97 season.

George O'Boyle

Striker

Place of Birth Northern Ireland

Height 1.79m

Date of Birth 14/12/67

Weight 76kg

When taking the Scottish First Division by storm in the emphatic way that St Johnstone did there were those who obviously played a major part in such success.

George O'Boyle is not a household name but after scoring over 20 goals in a season, earning his team promotion, he will now be looked upon as hot property.

The Northern Ireland international hopes to be considered by Bryan Hamilton in the future and is looking to add to the few caps he already has.

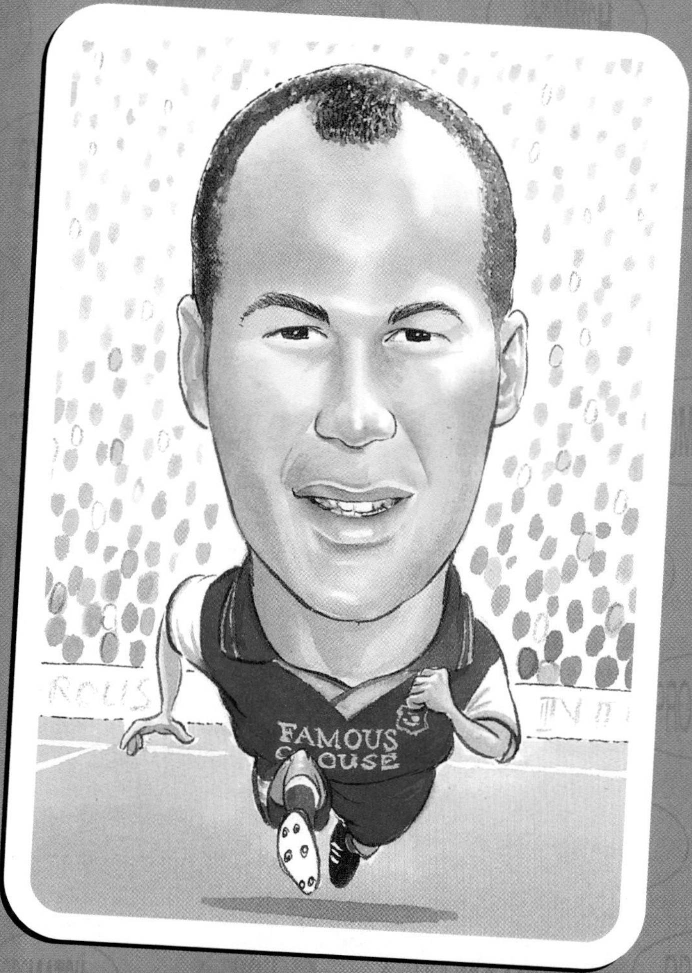

St. Johnstone

Gerry Britton

Position

Place of Birth Scotland

Height 1.80m

Date of Birth 20/10/70

Weight 78kg

At 25 Gerry now seems to have found a club where he can 'lay his boots'. The journeyman striker started his career at Celtic where he was way down the pecking order. He then moved around before being given his chance at Dunfermline.

Last season, when many had tipped Dunfermline for relegation, Gerry's goals and his partnership with Petrie and Smith made them a more sturdy team than East End Park teams of the past.

Dunfermline

THE ITALIAN SERIE A

Many say that the most exciting league in the world can now be found in the English Premiership, but the best players in the world are still to be found in the Scudetta along with some of the most exhilarating football.

Juventus once again proved that their talent and endeavour has made them probably the greatest side in the world and even the departure of Vialli and Ravanelli did not alter - European Cup Final aside - a near perfect season. The League was won convincingly and they again showed that they can go all the way to a European Cup Final, a double which many other sides find too hard to do. Allen Boksic proved that he could fill Ravanelli's boots and promising players such as Del Piero and Amuruso were quite outstanding.

With a team such as Juventus on the rise the other major giants in the Serie A, Milan, had their worst season for years. Their star-studded line-up looks as though it has some of the most talented players in the world, but off the field problems and a change in management meant that all they could manage was a mid-table finish and a dismal display in the Champions League, a competition they've often dominated.

Roy Hodgson departs for Blackburn leaving Inter on a sweet note having led them to the UEFA Cup final and a top three finish in the League. The Inter side has some superb players and the introduction of Youri Djourkaeff was another high point. But they were unable to cope fully with the demands of league and European competition.

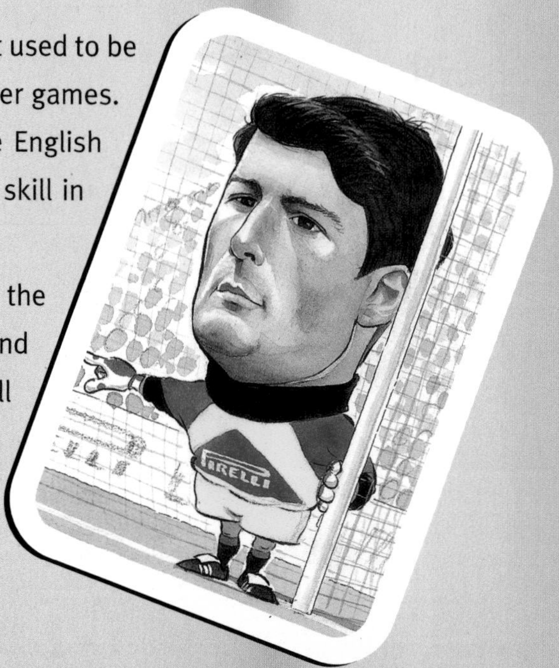

The Italian League has become much more open than it used to be with teams from the top and bottom having much closer games. There is still less tenacity and excitement than in the English Premiership, yet there is a higher level of quality and skill in the Serie A.

With Italy and England vying for that automatic spot in the World Cup qualifying group, will it be the strength and determination of the English lions that triumphs, or will the wondrous talents of the Italians, demonstrated in their awesome league, win the day?

THE SPANISH PRIMERA

With top players flocking to the Primera in recent years English fans enjoyed their first taste of Spanish football on television in 96/97. The excitement and the atmosphere the games produced have put us on the edge of our seats, as has the quality of the football and goals.

Real Madrid have once again proved that they still have the players to win the League even though Barcelona were their closest challengers once again. Yet while the goalscoring talent of Suker was to be marvelled at, it was the midfield that showed the quality that inspired the team. Seedorf, Raúl and Hierro all played to their highest capabilities as well as working hard for each other; their sweat and skill proved an unbeatable combination. The promise of Raúl is quite notable; his touch and vision at such a young age really is quite outstanding.

Barcelona were the main rivals to Real, yet Bobby Robson's side lacked consistency during the middle of the season and found themselves losing to teams much lower down the league. Yet there were good sides to their season; the form of players such as Ronaldo, Ammunike and young starlet De La Peña showed that they are still one of the top sides in Europe.

Athlético Madrid did not fulfil their early season potential and failed in the Champions League when Dutch champions Ajax tore them apart in Madrid.

Despite John Toshack's resignation, Deportivo La Coruña were to have a good season, clinching a UEFA Cup place. Surprise club Real Betis finished third, their highest position for years enabling them to show the rest of Europe what they can do next year.

The Spanish League seems to have grown stronger and stronger over the last few years with players from the Italian league moving to Spain, proving that it can be just as attractive a league and competition.

Paolo Maldini

Defender

Said by many to be the best defender in the world, and recently quoted as being worth £17 million, Paolo lived up to his reputation until his form dipped in the 96/97 season when his team did not fulfil their rich potential.

Even though his international place has never been in doubt, his place seems even more secure now - his dad is the manager!

A pin-up boy in Italy, Paolo has all the attributes for the perfect defender; pace, level headedness, quick thinking and, of course, strength in the tackle - whether centre-back, or his preferred position left-back, his presence guarantees a world class performance.

George Weah

Striker

Voted the best player in the world for the second year running, he is quite simply the best-ever player to come out of Africa and is ranked alongside Pele and Maradona by many critics.

When moving from France to Italy many doubted that he could come anywhere near the form he showed in French football but he captivated the minds of the Milan faithful by helping them to the Scudetta in his first season.

On the international scene George has made his own fairy tale by helping poverty stricken Liberia to maintain a team, funding them with the money he has earned over his career. A player who will never be forgotten.

Marcel Desailly

Midfielder

With attacking players such as Weah, Savicevic, Baggio and Albertini, Milan are so glad to have the defensive mind of Marcel Desailly who gives them steel in the centre of the midfield.

Simply nicknamed the 'Rock', advertising companies have even taken notice of the hard man and have used him in campaigns to demonstrate the Herculean power this man has on the football pitch.

For his country he is played in a preferred central defensive position which many see as a waste but, in over 55 appearances, he has played a major part in the success of the French football team. At 29 he still has quite a few more years ahead of him.

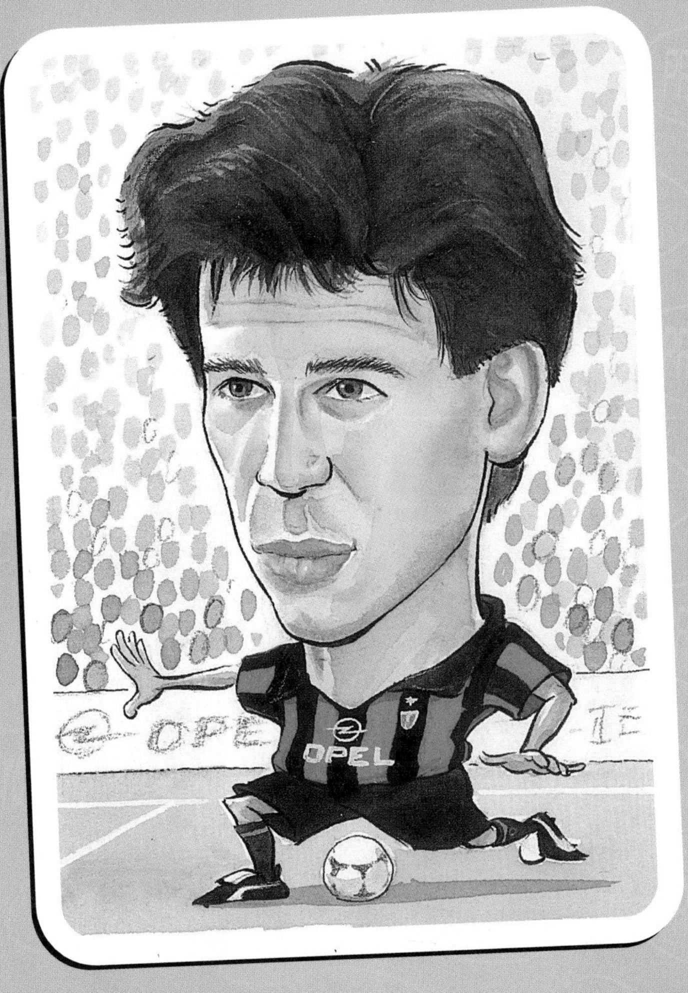

Demetrio Albertini

Midfielder

Many schoolkids around the world who aspire to the role of footballing playmaker look up to this man. His commanding presence on the ball, along with his astounding vision, make him the gifted player he is.

With Marcel Desailly in the centre of the midfield alongside Demetrio, it allows him a more attacking role, enabling him to get forward. This aspect of his game was shown to full effect when he scored over ten goals in the 95/96season - Milan's last title-winning year.

At the age of 25 he is now approaching 50 caps for his country, which is astonishing considering the changes the Italian management has undergone.

Paul Ince

Midfielder

Now in his late twenties, Paul is regarded as one of the most complete midfielders in the game. There's no doubt that playing in Italy has enhanced his game and, if he does return to the Premiership, English fans will see an even better player.

A player with all aspects of the game rolled into his play: with fabulous distribution, determination, never giving up a lost cause and an ability to get forward to score goals, it is so easy to see why the fans in Milan have made him one of their favourites.

Having now played over 30 international games, Paul is maybe one of THE most important players in his country's bid to reach the World Cup in France.

Ronaldo

Striker

The world's most expensive player now starts a fresh challenge as he joins Inter Milan in a £25 million deal from Spanish giants Barcelona.

Having scored 44 goals in as many games under Bobby Robson he became the most feared striker in Europe. His pace, power and finishing are second to none and he will go on to be one of the world's all time greats.

At only 20 years of age he is playing for his fourth club, yet he has proved a success everywhere and with a season in the Scudetta looming he can also show the rest of the world what he can do in the World Cup in France.

Jouri Djorkaeff

Midfielder

The departure of French players to Italy has seen many good imports but there's no doubt that the £5 million spent on Jouri was a sound investment.

Despite taking a while to distinguish himself in the French game he is now looked upon as the most dangerous player in the French national team. He is the major reason why Eric Cantona couldn't force himself into the team.

His speed and skill are quite devastating and have seen him score a goal every two games for his country. There has also been an impressive goal return on his Inter appearances. His first season in Italy saw him pick up some niggling injuries but, having overcome them, he is being widely tipped to be the player to watch in the 97/98 season.

Gianluca Pagliuca

Goalkeeper

Having reached the age of 30, it seems unlikely that he will add to his 30 international caps but there is no doubt that he is still rated one of the best goalkeepers in the Scudetta.

Once said to be the best goalkeeper in the world, Gianluca is a very energetic keeper whose reflexes are second to none but sometimes he can be too eccentric which can lead to criticism.

He will relish the thought of another challenge in European football next year and he hopes that he can recapture the form that saw him pull off some outstanding saves in the 1994 World Cup when he helped Italy to the final.

Angelo Peruzzi

Goalkeeper

Now establishing himself as the number one at Juventus he also has the honour of representing his country as the Italian goalkeeper. Not surprising really, as his performances have really been quite outstanding.

Angelo is an unusual keeper in his own right; even though he's very reliable he likes to punch the ball out and release attackers, which can be risky yet it is very effective.

Regarded as the best goalkeeper in Italy he is also considered to be up there with Seaman and Schmeichel as they vie to be acknowledged as the best keeper in Europe.

Zinidane Zidane

Midfielder

The 'Z' man, as he is known, has become an instant success with the crowds in Turin and with his French compatriot, Didier Deschamps, they have formed probably the most dangerous midfield in Italy.

After having one of the seasons of his life for Bordeaux he was snapped up by Juventus in a multi-million pound deal. He has settled in easily, unlike others who've seemed disillusioned by the move.

He showed many English fans why he is so highly rated with some very impressive performances in the Champions League against Manchester United when he took hold of the midfield and, with devastating vision, tore the United defence apart.

Alessandro Del Piero

Striker

Alessandro has been tipped as the next Roberto Baggio and there can be few better players to base your game on. There are similarities in stature and ability, though Alessandro has maybe more pace and lasts the 90 minutes better than Baggio.

At only 22 he has now become a regular in the Juventus side and is seen as a player to turn to whenever something special is needed.

He has already performed at international level four times and the Italian manager feels that Del Piero has the potential to be one of Italy's all-time greats. A natural matchwinner.

Juventus

Alan Boksic

Striker

In his Lazio days he was never seen as a player who would score enough goals to make him one of the most prolific goalscorers in the Scudetta yet he was never the main striker with Signori and Casiraghi overshadowing him.

When bought to replace Fabrizio Ravanelli eyebrows were raised, yet he has proved everyone wrong. In a Juventus shirt, he has shown that he really is an extremely talented player; with his pace, strength and incredibly good touch for a man over six feet tall.

Now forcing his way back into the Croatian side, he can partner Davor Suker in what is quite possibly the most talented forward line in European football.

Christian Karambeau

Midfielder

French international Christian has made a real impact in his first full session in Serie A. The deadly dreadlocked dynamo hopes o go one step further than last year and help his team mount a Championship challenge.

The stockily built Frenchman can operate either in midfield or in defence, but his preferred position is at right wing-back, where he is at his best, both attacking and defending.

With his silky skills and tough attitude, he is an asset to both club and country, and could well go on to be one of France's greatest players.

Vincenzo Montella

Striker

After struggling to find his mark for many years, languishing in the lower leagues, he was given his chance in the Scudetta where he finished amongst the top marksmen in the league.

After a spell with Genoa he had ambitions to show what he could do at a higher level and he had an especially good season in the UEFA Cup.

He is very fast and has plenty of ability, but crucially, he has the right temperament, something other Italian strikers have often lacked.

Sampdoria

Sinisa Mihailovic

Midfielder

The Yugoslavian international has one of the sweetest right feet in the world with an amazing ability to put an awesome curve on the ball.

Having joined Sampdoria a few seasons back he did not initially make the impact he would have liked, yet he now has the admiration of many of the fans in Italy.

His country has suffered terribly and he hopes he can relieve the gloom by helping his national team qualify for the World Cup finals. They have a good chance and, if they were to reach the finals, they would certainly not be underestimated, especially with Sinisa in the middle of the park.

Roberto Mancini

Striker

A legend in Italy, where he defies his critics every season. When he's dismissed as being 'too old' or 'finished', he produces some breathtaking football and shows why he is still one of the best strikers in the world.

Now, at the age of the 32, the years are creeping up on him yet there is still much football left in the 'old man' as shown in the 96/97 season when he had one of his best seasons ever.

A true leader at the front of the park who reads the game wonderfully. He would agree that he won't add to his 37 caps yet he can look back on a wonderful career when he has won almost every title there is to win.

AS Roma

Daniel Fonseca

Striker

When arriving at Roma three seasons ago little was known about the Uruguayan international and even though his team have been labelled one of the underachievers of Italian football, his partnership with Able Balbo is one of the most dangerous in the Scudetta, giving Roma that South American touch.

His country have always been in the shadow of Brazil and Argentina yet they now look as though they could challenge them both and with Daniel leading the attack there are few other strikers that you'd want in your forward line.

Fiorentina

Gabriel Batistuta

Striker

For a striker to remain at an Italian club for over five years is quite unusual. Yet Gabriel has always seemed happy at Fiorentina where he has, on two occasions, finished top scorer in the Scudetta.

The fans have rewarded their idol by placing a model of the player in the stadium; he is adored by his fans.

When on form he is one of the best strikers in the world yet he has a tendency to go in and out of games. But there's no doubting his ability and, for club and country, he is prolific in front of goal.

Pierluigi Casiraghi

Striker

Once regarded as the whipping boy of the Lazio crowd, Pierluigi played second fiddle to Boksic for years but now he has the crowd on his side and is first choice both for his club and his country.

His pace and height are often dealt with yet many defenders are surprised by this big man's amazing first touch and he uses that to his advantage.

He hopes to play over 50 games for Italy and, with 45 caps, he is nearly there. Yet the onus is on him to help Italy win a major championship. It will be hard as Italy have struggled for many years to find the right formula up front.

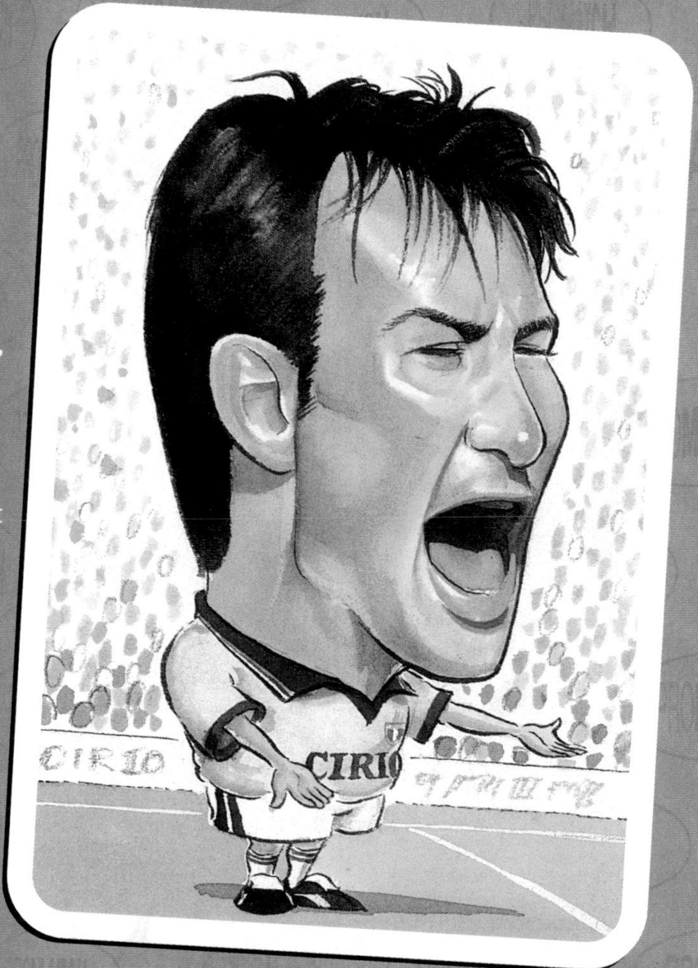

Lazio

Dino Baggio

Midfielder

Once he lived in the shadow of his older brother, Roberto, yet now he seems to have taken his place in the Italian side and his reputation is growing.

He is a wonderful footballer with superb distribution and a great first touch. Having played for Juventus and now Parma, he is learning all the time and is reaching the peak of his career.

Many English fans will remember him for his inspiring performances in the 1994 World Cup; he will almost certainly be able to have another go at repeating those performances in France next year.

Parma

Diego Simeone

Midfielder

The diminutive Argentinian playmaker has had another outstanding season in the Primera yet there have been times when his team-mates have not been on his wavelength. Yet in the 95/96 season, Diego's passes were often read perfectly by his team-mates and the title was won.

He is such an important player for Atlético that, when he doesn't tick, the team finds it hard to score goals.

At 26 he is at the peak of his career and it has been rumoured that a move to an Italian club is about to take place. He is just the sort of player who could revel in a league where technique is so important.

Kiko

Striker

When winning the league in the 95/96 season there was no-one more important than Kiko. He was rarely noticed until Atlético won their title but he is now one of the most dangerous marksmen in Spain.

He has forced his way into the national team, where he has become one of the first team strikers because he can score just as prolifically at international level; scoring a goal every two games for his country.

He's adored by the fans yet he was guilty of missing some simple chances in the Champions League where they were narrowly beaten by Ajax despite having the chances to progress.

Milinko Pantic

Midfielder

A real late starter in his footballing career, he really only started to shine at age 28, but what a player he has proved to be for Atlético!

Milinko's a midfielder who loves to get forward and score goals and, on one memorable night, he scored four goals in Barcelona but he still saw his side lose the game!

The Yugoslavian international has made a real name for himself in Madrid and is thought to be one of the hottest properties around but, at 30, he does not have age on his side if he wants to go on to better things in his career.

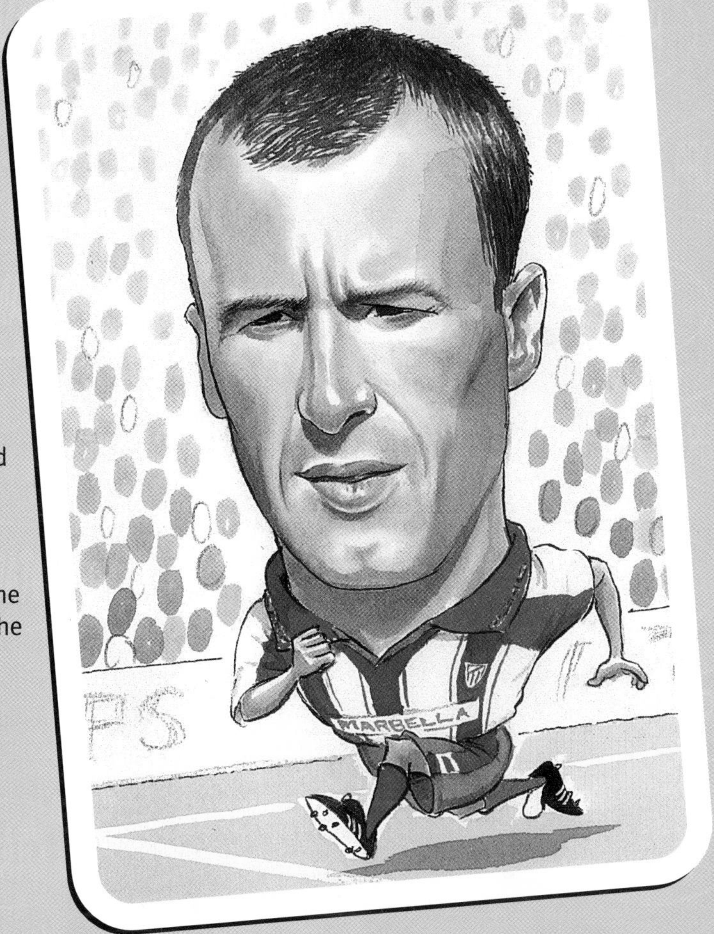

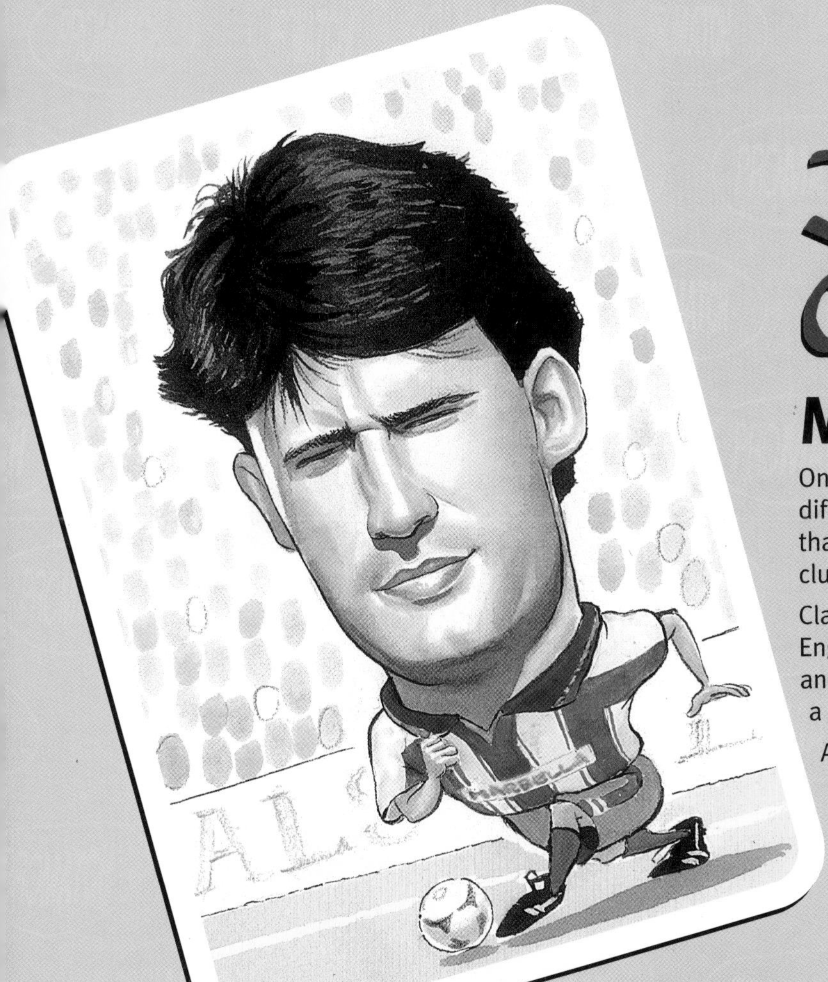

José Luis Caminero

Midfielder

One of Spain's real all-round players who has many different attributes to his game; it's not surprising that he's nearly always first on the team sheets of his club and national teams.

Classed as a defensive midfielder, he proved to English fans in Euro 96 that he loves to get forward and score goals though, with Atlético he does play in a deeper role.

Along with Simeone and Pantic in the middle of the park the three form one of the best midfields in Europe, yet it is Caminero who's always talked about as being most important to the side because of his enthusiasm and inspiration.

Miguel Angel Nadal

Defender

The 'Beast', as he is known in the Spanish game, has had another outstanding season at the back for Barcelona, once again being probably the most consistent player for his club.

With much interest surrounding him from Italian and English clubs, there were strong thoughts that he was leaving Spain but when offered a new contract it seemed to revitalise him. Bobby Robson really has got the best out of him.

He has a tremendous turn of pace which can match the speediest of strikers. He's also so powerful that his presence at the back is sometimes too much for forwards and he simply brushes them off the ball. He's already a Nou Camp legend.

Emmanuel Ammunike

Midfielder

Despite being an unknown commodity when brought to Barcelona he has really been quite a star since his arrival.

When Bobby Robson was bringing in world class players, such as Ronaldo and Luis Enrique, there was little known about the miniature Nigerian but now he is thought to be one of the most dangerous players when the ball is at his feet.

A gifted player with startling skills, he learnt his trade from the African players around the world such as Okocha, Yeboah and Amokachi and there will now be youngsters in Africa and Spain who will look up to Emmanuel as an inspiration.

Luis Enrique

Midfielder

When transferred from Real Madrid in the summer of 96 for a fee of around £5 million, it meant one of Spain's finest young players was moving from one of Spain's giants to another. Real's loss is most certainly Barcelona's gain.

His disciplinary record on the pitch is not as impressive as his footballing skills but if he can continue putting in top class performances then the fans won't really concern themselves over a few rash challenges.

Despite being so influential for his club, Luis, like many Spanish players, cannot seem to perform at such a high level when a big international tournament arrives. In Euro 96 he was one of the major disappointments as his excellent club form deserted him.

Barcelona

Iván de la Peña

Midfielder

The promising midfielder made a name for himself in his first full season in the Barcelona side with some quite breathtaking performances.

At only 20 years of age he has shown that his skill and tenacity makes up for his limited experience. Recognisable in the middle of the park with his diminutive figure and shaven head, many have tipped him to become one of Spain's top players.

He is starting to be recognised also by the Spanish coach and will almost certainly feature in the World Cup set-up.

Jacques Songo'o

Goalkeeper

The Cameroon international goalkeeper is now finally acknowledged as one of the great shotstoppers in the world and even though he is not first choice keeper anymore he is regarded as one of the great characters in the Spanish Primera.

The 32 year-old keeper played in the World Cup of 94 in America where he was let down by many of his defenders, as they failed to recapture the form of the Italia 90 team.

He has hinted that he would like to finish his career in his home country so he may move on during the summer.

Mauro Silva

Midfielder

At 28 he seems to have been around for ages yet the Brazilian international is still at the top of his game and has insisted that he wants to play for as long as he is able.

Many remember him as being the linchpin in the Brazilian midfield in the 1994 World Cup where he performed quite superbly, attracting rave notices around the world.

At Deportivo he has not had the happiest of times yet John Toshack realised his potential when he brought him there and Mauro is still one of the best midfielders in the Spanish game.

Deportivo de la Coruña

Corentine Martins

Midfielder

The French dynamo had a quite superb first season in the Primera where he slotted naturally into the Spanish game.

After impressing many clubs around the world with his devastating performances for Auxerre he was snapped up by Deportivo in a multi-million pound deal.

His appearances for France have been limited, yet, at 27, he has time to add to his 13 caps and will almost certainly be part of the national squad to play in the World Cup.

Rivaldo

Midfielder

One of the most skilful players in the world and despite having injury problems, he has played a major part in his side gaining a UEFA Cup place.

He is still young at 24 and has time to get into the Brazilian side but he must really toughen himself up if he is to be considered.

There has been talk of a move to Italy or even to the Premiership, where he's seen that Juninho has been an exceptional success. Many see Rivaldo in the same mould as the Middlesbrough man.

Raúl

Midfielder

Tipped to be the best all-round player in the world, Raúl is only 19 and has a secure first team place in the Real Madrid line-up. He has the ability to play in defence, midfield or attack and is beginning to get recognition from the international team.

In the past season he was played behind strikers, Mijatovic and Suker, where it was his consistency that led to another succesful season for his team.

One can only gaze at the unbelievable progress of this teen sensation and it is really in his hands if he wants to become one of the all-time great players.

Clarence Seedorf

Midfielder

Being groomed at the academy of Ajax meant that Clarence had the best education in football and, after a year of impressing many playing alongside Paul Ince at Inter Milan, ex-AC Milan coach, Fabio Capello, brought the Dutch playmaker to Real Madrid.

His manager commented: 'If you want him to pass it to any player on the pitch, it will be on their feet, perfectly weighted.' I can only agree and say that he is quite a remarkable passer and has incredible vision.

A player whose career can only go on to greater things and, having already played for three of the top sides in the world, he must be regarded as one of the top midfielders in football.

Fernando Hierro

Midfielder

Club captain, captain of his country and all-round inspiration for his team-mates and fans, he epitomises the hard working footballer whose strength and determination make him so valuable to whatever team he is playing for.

With Real being noticeably more successful over the last few seasons, it is no coincidence that it has coincided with the amazing form of Fernando.

With a shot of quite startling power, he notches his fair share of goals and does a lot of ground work which goes unnoticed. A player who will surely be remembered for a long time in Spain.

Real Madrid

Davor Suker

Striker

A player who really showed what he can do in the European Championships of 1996. Terry Venables regarded Suker as the most dangerous frontman with the quickest football mind in Europe.

A multi-million pound move saw him cross from Sevilla to Real Madrid, forming an egocentric partnership with Pedrag Mijatovic that sometimes produces some of the most dynamic moves or can go infuriatingly wrong.

Although inconsistent, on his day Suker can show why Fabio Capello paid well over £5 million for a 30 year-old player and, although a late developer in the game, he is quite capable of achieving great heights.

Athletic Bilbao

Julen Guerrero

Striker

At only 22, he has over 25 national caps under his belt and eight goals; a talent that has not been ignored by Spanish coach Clemente.

The nippy striker has been said to be the same sort of player as Gary Lineker but despite such a flattering compliment, Julen has the ambition to become a legend in his own right.

He certainly has the talent but much depends on whether he accepts that at the the young age of 22 he is still learning, and will have to accept the highs and lows of football.

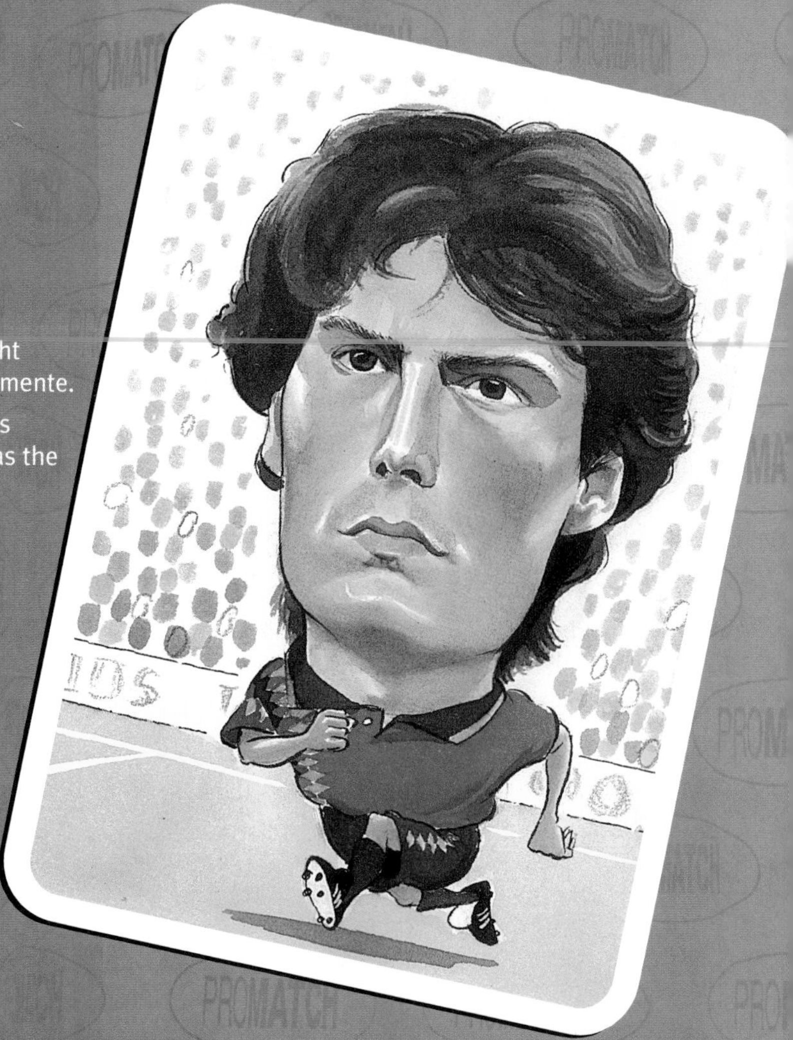

S.D. Compostela

Christopher Ohen

Striker

A real unknown quantity around the world but he has exploded on the scene in the Compostela team, who will be lucky to hold on to such a player as Christopher.

Following in the footsteps of Amokachi and Yekini, Christopher now plays in the national team and is hoping to lead the strike force into the World Cup of 98.

A real powerhouse who leads the line well, he has the speed, agility and strength to made a real name for himself in the coming seasons.

Finidi

Midfielder

The Nigerian midfielder has really made an impact since joining Real Betis and he is just the sort of player that they have needed after playing second fiddle to teams such as Barcelona and Real Madrid.

The former Ajax man made a name for himself in Amsterdam where his performances gave him African Player of the Year, a European Cup winner's medal and rave reviews around the world.

At 26 he is no longer the youngster that graced the fields of Betis and Amsterdam yet he still has plenty of years left to make a name for himself in Spain.

Goran Vlaovic

Striker

After the European Championships in England there was much controversy over which club Goran actually belonged to. He was finally given his chance to play at Spanish giants, Valencia, where he continued the form that he showed in Euro 96 for Croatia.

A real livewire with great speed and an eye for a goal. He's played in Italy and now in Spain and, bearing in mind the experiences of other Croatian players, it would be no surprise if he moved to another club in another country.

WORLD CUP

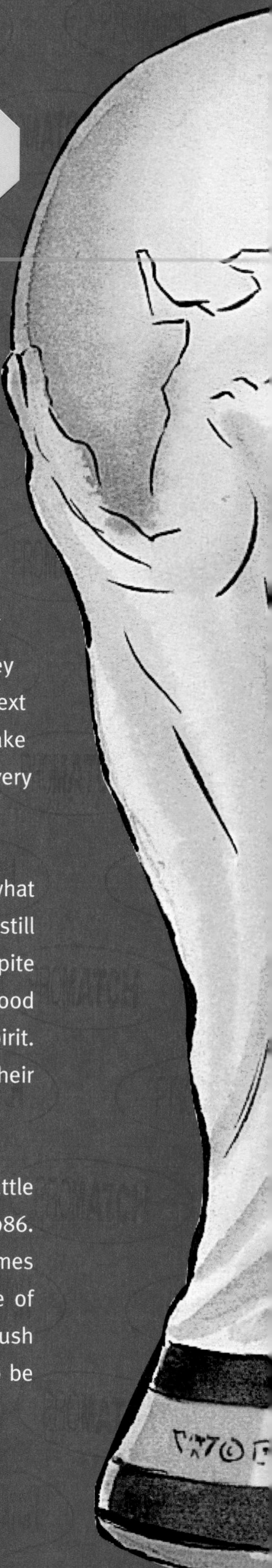

With the World Cup approaching many teams around the world are beginning to feel the strain and the pressures of qualification; the United Kingdom teams in particular.

Since Glenn Hoddle's arrival he has preferred a much more orthodox style of playing than that of his predecessor, Terry Venables. Yet Hoddle's team has only lost one competitive game against the Italians; unfortunately it will most probably prove to be the match that sees England unable to finish top of their group. Yet the chances are, if they win the remainder of their games, they will finish as one of the best runners-up which will see them go to France next year. Players such as Shearer, Ince, Beckham and Fowler are all ready to take centre stage in a World Cup competition and, if England qualify, there is every chance that they can do well.

Scotland are in a more comfortable position than the English and have what seems to be an easier group. Yet the Swedish are unpredictable and could still mount a late challenge. Craig Brown has done wonders with his side and, despite lacking the resources and players that the English have, he has brought a good bunch of players together and they have gelled, creating a terrific team spirit. Collins, McAllister, Ferguson and Hendry are all top quality players and with their experience and talent they can help those around them.

For the other home nations clubs it seems as though it is going to be a hard battle to try and get into the World Cup. Eire will miss out for the first time since 1986. Mick McCarthy never really seemed to get a settled side and lost some vital games to some of the lesser known countries. Wales never really looked capable of qualification with a very average defence and only a few shining players, like Rush and Hughes - both nearing the end of their careers - there never seemed to be

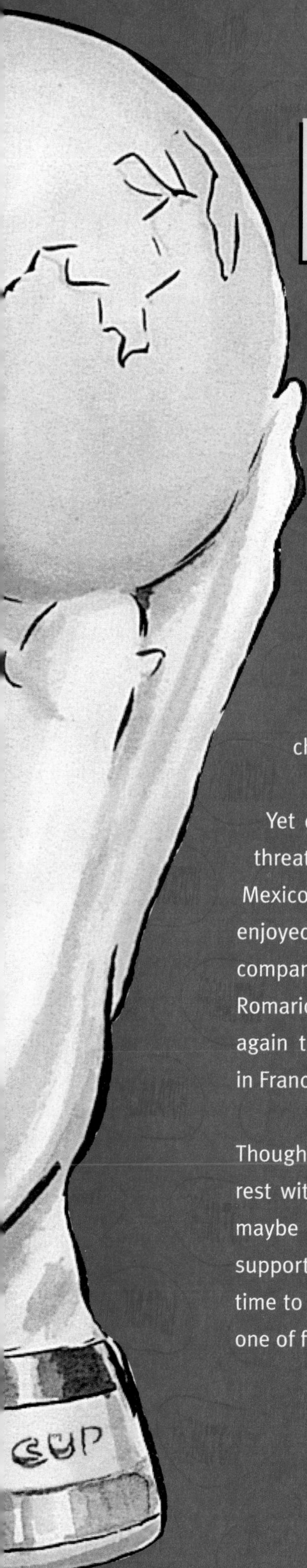

PREVIEW

sufficient team spirit to replace the lack of quality. Northern Ireland once again failed to deliver yet Bryan Hamilton is building a side with very few resources and there are possibilities for his team in the future. They could well be a stronger force in the next European Championships.

With qualification to be settled by the end of the year there look to be few surprises. The Germans, Italians, Dutch and Romanians look as strong as ever and there is little surprise with the way other teams are playing on the other continents. Argentina and Colombia look strong as does the USA, also Terry Venables and his Australian side seem to have a chance of qualifying.

Yet despite the emergence of the African nations and the strong European threat, the Brazilians still look a class apart. When the world champions crushed Mexico 4-0 in May even the Mexican coach was moved to say how much he enjoyed his side's annihilation. Having been sponsored by a major sports company, Brazil tour the world and show off their skills. Players such as Ronaldo, Romario, and Roberto Carlos are the best in the world at what they do and once again they are going to be an awesome force when it comes to the crunch in France 98.

Though the Brazilians do look an outstanding outfit our main hopes (and fears!) rest with the British teams. England and Scotland should both qualify though maybe England will be the main British threat. But both sets of passionate supporters will be vying for success, especially the English – 32 years is a long time to wait for a trophy on the international scene when you're supposed to be one of football's major powers.

Levinson Books would like to thank:
Heather Ellis, Kristy Flowers, Warren Goldberg, Marc Green,
James Griffiths, Steve Holmes, James Lamb and Louise Rooney
for all their help in the production of this book.

Editor's Note:
The final date for compiling this book was June 1 1997.
All reasonable efforts were made to ensure that the data was accurate at that time.
Player transfers and/or managerial changes after that date were, of course, beyond our control.